# My Supernatural Life

Dr. David Craig

Word 2 Word
Publishing

Seeing the Future by Dreams and Visions
Dr. David Craig
Copyright © 2018 by David Craig Ministries

All scripture is taken from the King James Version of the Bible unless otherwise noted. Scripture quotations marked NKJV are taken from the New King James Version. NKJV Copyright © 1982 by Thomas Nelson, Inc. Used by permission. All rights reserved. NLT: Scripture quotations marked NLT are taken from the Holy Bible, New Living Translation, copyright 1996. Used by permission of Tyndale House Publishers, Inc., Wheaton, Illinois 60189. All rights reserved. MSG: Scripture marked MSG taken from The Message. Copyright 1993, 1994, 1995, 1996, 2000, 2001, 2002. Used by permission of NavPress Publishing Group.

ISBN-13: 978-1987565553
ISBN-10: 198756555X

First Edition Printed May 2018
Printed in the United States of America

Author Contact Info:
Life Church
PO Box 1652
Sikeston, Mo 63801
David@dcmlifechurch.org
www.dcraig.org
#dcm
#davidcraigministries
Davidcraigministries.yourstreamlive.com

Word2 Word

Publishing, Sikeston, MO
word2wordministries@gmail.com

Cover Design by Brant Hutchcraft
brantphotodesign@yahoo.com

# Dedication

I dedicate this to all who see beyond the veil. Strange as we may seem to others, we who are blessed to see beyond the veil are God's normal. God is a Spirit. All of mankind created in the image and likeness of God are spirits. All Born Again Christians, new creatures in Christ Jesus, who have recreated spirits, are networked into the Holy Spirit. God's Sprit communicates with our spirit as He leads and guides us into all truth. God's Word is spirit and God communicates with us primarily through His Word, secondly by human, messengers and beyond that with dreams, visions, angels (supernatural messengers) and occasionally by a direct visitation from the Lord Jesus Himself.

# Table of Contents

Introduction

PART 1 - Pre-Salvation Dreams and Visions

PART 2 - Post-Salvation Dreams and Visions

# Introduction

God has been so very good to me to share His will for the immediate as well as for the future. I have lived in this heavenly supernatural flow so much that I needed to give God thanks for what I could have easily take for granted. As clearly and accurately as I can recall, I have recorded these events to inspire the hope of God in you and renew hope in me. God is so much better than we can imagine.

**Supernatural:** of or relating to an order of existence beyond the invisible observable universe, especially relating to God. I have lived a supernatural life in the kingdom of God since my first remembrance of attending a church at four years of age. No one knew my attendance at the community church in Clover Bend, Arkansas would open my life to supernatural realities beyond the realities of this natural world. The supernatural life of dreams, visions and having angels around to protect me was my normal life, and I thought this was normal life for everyone.

Originally, all created things came into being by God's supernatural power. Today, most people have some information about the supernatural world of darkness but know very little about the supernatural life available from God. It is the will of God for the church and Christians individually to live in the supernatural world of the Kingdom of God. It is God's way, and we should know more about it. Hopefully, Christianity will soon realize it cannot accomplish its mission without living in the supernatural possibilities of the Kingdom of God.

# Introduction

God has been so very good to me to share His will for the immediate as well as for the future. I have lived in this heavenly supernatural flow so much that I needed to give God thanks for what I could have easily take for granted. As clearly and accurately as I can recall, I have recorded these events to inspire the hope of God in you and renew hope in me. God is so much better than we can imagine.

**Supernatural:** of or relating to an order of existence beyond the invisible observable universe, especially relating to God. I have lived a supernatural life in the kingdom of God since my first remembrance of attending a church at four years of age. No one knew my attendance at the community church in Clover Bend, Arkansas would open my life to supernatural realities beyond the realities of this natural world. The supernatural life of dreams, visions and having angels around to protect me was my normal life, and I thought this was normal life for everyone.

Originally, all created things came into being by God's supernatural power. Today, most people have some information about the supernatural world of darkness but know very little about the supernatural life available from God. It is the will of God for the church and Christians individually to live in the supernatural world of the Kingdom of God. It is God's way, and we should know more about it. Hopefully, Christianity will soon realize it cannot accomplish its mission without living in the supernatural possibilities of the Kingdom of God.

# Part 1

# Pre-Salvation Dreams and Visions

# 1

# 1952:
# My First Time Attending
# a Church Service

In the spring of 1952, before I became five years of age, a neighboring family took me to church. It is my earliest memory of attending a church service. My dad was a veteran of WWII and had returned from the war with much pain and sorrow in his soul, but as far as I know, he did not seek God's restoration as a Christian. At least he did not get his family involved in a local church.

The family that took me to church was all cleaned up, dressed and seated in their horse or mule-drawn, four-wheel wagon. I, on the other hand, was barefoot and dirty from playing in the middle of the dirt road. No hard surfaced or gravel roads existed off the beaten path in Clover Bend, Arkansas in 1952. I had never heard of a sandbox, but I did have experience playing in the dirt, dust when dry and mud when wet. When the roads were dry, the dirt became like talcum powder as it was pounded by the wheels of vehicles and wagons and the hooves of animals. It was easy to create a dust storm by throwing it up into the air and letting the finer particles drift back down on top of you. That was what I was doing on the morning of my divine appointment.

Do not be alarmed! My parents were not neglecting me. Playing in the middle of the road was completely safe, as very few vehicles passed by our house. People riding horses or farm equipment being pulled slowly along the road by a horse was common. It was a very slow paced and safe existence.

Surely it was an inspiration of the Holy Spirit within the man to ask permission from my dad to take me to church with his family. I believe I was the only person from our family that attended church that Sunday. Sadly I do not remember the name of the man nor was I acquainted with his family, but I am eternally grateful that he obeyed the voice of God that particular day. I can still visualize the man and my dad looking at each other and conversing among themselves, the man in the wagon in the middle of the road and my dad near the house. I assume they were discussing the possibility of me attending church with them, and it was surely settled in the affirmative. The man reached down over the wagon wheel and picked me up into the wagon.

This little dirty urchin was about to be introduced to a supernatural world of the kingdom of God. Little did I know that from that day onward I would see the future by dreams, visions, and visitations from supernatural beings, angels that were assigned to reveal things to me and to protect me.

In recent years I was shown a picture of the building. It was an abandoned one-room school building that a start-up community church was using for their services until they could purchase property and build their own sanctuary. I do not remember the trip to or from the church. Nor do I remember being inside the church walls. All I remember was playing outside the building, around the trees and from time to time looking into the front door. When I peeked in, I saw the backs of people as they were looking forward toward a speaker who was facing them. I do not remember a sermon, nor anyone praying for me, nor even speaking to me about the kingdom of God, but God attached Himself to my life from that very day.

While attending church for the first time, God surely did something special for me. From that day forward, I have lived a supernatural life in communication with Creator God. I began to see into the realm of the spirit by supernatural means. I could and can see behind the veil into the realm of the spirit at the same time I see

2

natural things with my five senses, taste, touch, sight, smell, sound. Please understand, I have no control of this ability nor do I ask for it, but I can yield to it as I am inclined by the Holy Spirit Also, by the same means, I can see events that will come to pass in the future. Before my salvation in May 1977, I had no understanding of how these things happened, but I now know it has always been the Holy Ghost revealing things to me.

In those early years, until July 1957, I heard things from within the realm of the spirit, and I lived in the presence of angels.

> Matthew 18:10 (KJV)
> 10 Take heed that ye despise not one of these little ones; for I say unto you, that in heaven their angels do always behold the face of my Father which is in heaven.

These angels were not my playmates but creatures that were around me, probably all the time. When I say creatures, I do not mean to imply they were odd to me. They seemed to be like grown men, but I do not remember distinct physical facial features. Sometimes I could see them as they were relaxing close by, like men leaning against a wall, sitting on the tailgate of a pickup truck or squatting down by the trunk of a tree. Sometimes they hovered over or around me or looked over my shoulder. I could hear them talking but did not understand what they were saying. However, it felt very normal, like being around adults gathered around talking among themselves while the children played quietly nearby.

Sometimes these creatures wore bright clothing that seemed to shimmer as objects viewed through the heat waves coming from the ground. Cornelius, the centurion, recorded in Acts 10-11 that an angel appeared to him in response to his almsgiving and prayers. The angel was sent from God to give him a message to locate the

3

Apostle Peter. The angel said that Peter would come to tell him words whereby he and his household might be saved.

In Acts 10:30, Cornelius described the angel that appeared to him as a man in bright clothing.

> Acts 10:30 (KJV)
> [30] And Cornelius said, Four days ago I was fasting until this hour; and at the ninth hour I prayed in my house, and, behold, a man stood before me in bright clothing,

I know by experience the clothing Cornelius described. I could see the unseen, or at least what was unseen by most people. It was my normal life, and I thought everybody was living just like me. Gradually, it became evident to me that very few people are privileged to experience this supernatural life. The supernatural life, as I describe it, seemed to be the natural life for me, and it is to this day.

I did not know how to explain to anyone how I was hearing what I heard or seeing what I saw, but it was as real to me as everything happening in the natural realm. Sometimes people thought I was a little odd, and yet I thought they were the odd ones because they were unaware of the supernatural realm we live in. I was mystified that they were oblivious to what I saw and heard. All of us, especially Christians, should be living a supernatural life in the Spirit in what we refer to as the natural world.

# 2

# In the early 1950s:
# Visions of God in Grade School

During our early years on the farm in Essex Missouri, the supernatural life I experienced was developing, and I was quite relaxed living it because I thought this was the natural life of all humans. Dreams were commonplace with me, and I occasionally saw visions. Once by a vision from God, I was shown that a high school girl that had befriended me would die.

> John 16:13 (KJV)
> "Howbeit when he, the Spirit of truth, is come, he will guide you into all truth: for he shall not speak of himself; but whatsoever he shall hear, that shall he speak: and he will shew you things to come."

The vision I saw did not scare me. Though I do not remember having experienced the death of a human prior to this one. It was simply a piece of information to warn me of what was to come. I do not recall her name, nor can I describe her. But I liked her. She seemed concerned for my welfare and let me sit with her on the bus. She died within a few months after I had the vision. I was not surprised at her passing, but I was saddened for losing a friend.

# 3

# Hell was beaten into me

Before I share the following stories of a dark twenty years of my life, I need to pre-empt them by sharing some good stories.

I now see clearly that when a devil is allowed to come into your life, whether you have invited him or not, and he is not driven out, he will drive you into greater and greater insanity. The devil surely entered and terribly scarred my dad's life in WWII. He returned to his family convinced he was a murderer. War can cause not only death to the body but the inward man as well, and it did my dad. He had made much progress in his recovery up until 1957. That year our family was destroyed financially, and Dad was thoroughly destroyed in his inward man.

My dad's inward man collapse [commonly referred to as mental collapse] allowed a devil to take him over, and through his actions, the devil had free access to us. That devil took over our family and wanted us to kill one another.

Many who have been raised in similar situations or with greater demonic influence and control, did not have the good fortune of God's protection. They died young or were imprisoned. Their lives and their families' lives were breeding grounds for even more darkness.

Dad had many good traits. As Dad exceeded seventy years, he began to share more stories of his life. He was an athlete and had some good notoriety as a football player from Blytheville Arkansas High School through his sophomore year in college.

He had a saved the lives of a few people. He saved a young girl from drowning in a pool. He saved a crippled friend who was drowning trying to swim across the cold water of a Bauxite pit. He saved a mother and her child out of a burning house. About that particular incident, he said, "David, that house was engulfed in flames, but when I heard the woman screaming for help, I went in with no concern of my own life." Then he asked, "Why would I do that?"

He probably had a call of God on his life but Satan, the cruel taskmaster, found a way to break him by war and by financial collapse. Those two traps were enough to turn him into a different man. All our family may have had a call of God to fivefold ministry, but only two out of the six children had the good fortune to hear the call of God and follow it.

Our blessing and saving grace was that one of our family friends prayed for us and our salvation.

Wanda was a member of the Assembly of God Church, Clover Bend Arkansas. She met our family after WWII in 1946, when dad took a teaching position in their public school. Wanda's husband, Ralph, and Dad became very good friends. Wanda was very gentle and did not like Dad at first. She viewed him as very rough and coarse, but as she visited with our family more, she began to see a softer side of him.

Wanda began to pray for us in 1946 and continued to pray for us till her death above ninety years of age.


Dad did save my life on two occasions; once before he was broken and once after he was a Christian.

I was four or less when he saved me from a mean Jersey bull. I had gotten into the barn lot and quickly met by my adversary, the bull. The bull had his head down and was pawing the dirt, preparing to run over me. Dad must have seen me go into the lot or heard the bull bellowing. He appeared out of the blue and tossed me back onto the gate. The bull charged him. He stepped forward with a 'single tree' in his hands, hit the bull in the top of the head and knocked the bull out. The bull's legs spread out to the side as he fell to the ground. Later, dad returned the bull to the college from where he had borrowed him.

Another time he saved me from being decapitated by a variable speed pulley system on a 750 Massey Ferguson Combine. I heard a noise in a pulley bearing and was following the sound with my ears to locate the source. Without realizing my predicament, I had placed my head inside the belt loop of the variable speed drive pulleys. With just one false move, I would have been killed. God graced him to come behind me without startling me and snatch me straight away from death.

The twenty years between 1957, when hell was beaten into me by my dad, and 1977 when hell was driven out of me by Jesus Christ, life was miserable. Becoming a new creature in Christ Jesus has been my true salvation, spirit, soul, and body. Between these two life-changing events, I grew to hate my dad with a dark passion of devilish vengeance and murder. After becoming a Christian, I slowly began to bear the fruit of love, and I learned to love my dad. Odd as it may seem, I had always wanted to love him when he seemed to hate us. All of my family did everything we could to please him and prove that we wanted his approval but to no avail.

Learning that [agape] love is an act of the will and not initiated by emotion, or intimate feelings has allowed me to overcome hatred and vengeance. Many painful memories and scars no longer hinder me, and some very good memories have returned to bless me. I had always honored and respected dad as much as possible, but I learned to love him by an act of my will and the supernatural help of the Holy Ghost.

Love is truly a fruit of the Spirit and not a gift of the Spirit. Like any fruit that has been tested by all the elements of an adverse life during its development so is the love of God. Like natural fruit, it can have a delicious flavor in the end. On the outside, it may look like it has been through WWIII but the inside is full of supernatural life.

Though you may not have noticed, the Apostle Paul suffered much and gradually bore the fruit of love. I like his exhortations.

> Ephesians 3:14-21 (KJV)
> [14] For this cause I bow my knees unto the Father of our Lord Jesus Christ, [15] Of whom the whole family in heaven and earth is named, [16] That he would grant you, according to the riches of his glory, to be strengthened with might by his Spirit in the inner man; [17] That Christ may dwell in your hearts by faith; that ye, being rooted and grounded in love, [18] May be able to comprehend with all saints what is the breadth, and length, and depth, and height; [19] And to know the love of Christ, which passeth knowledge, that ye might be filled with all the fulness of God. [20] Now unto him that is able to do exceeding abundantly above all that we ask or think, according to the power that worketh in us, [21] Unto him be glory in the church by Christ Jesus throughout all ages, world without end. Amen.

In *The Heart of Paul*, a relational paraphrase of the New Testament, author Ben Campbell Johnson has a great paraphrase of these same verses. Verses 18-20 says, "I hope that you will be able to grasp with all God-persons **the multidimensional love of God—** a love broad enough to include everybody, long enough to reach to the ends of the earth, **deep enough to unify our human fragmentation,** and high enough to reach the very heart of God. Actually, I want you to know the love of Christ which is beyond knowing. **Experiencing love like this,** may you be overwhelmed with the awareness of the presence of God."

Before the initial beating, when hell was beaten into me, the God Life, the supernatural life of living in the kingdom of God, was very peaceful for me. I had never experienced any other life. I lived this "Wonderful Life," until age ten. At that young age, in 1957, Hell was beaten <u>into</u> me in a moment of time. My peaceful soul was removed and replaced by a devil during the beating. I did not know how to resist the devil. He came in without my permission, to destroy the life God had opened for me when I attended my first church service. The devil did not leave until I was born again in May 1977.

The 1957 flooding and destruction in Southeast Missouri triggered insanity in my dad that prevailed for two decades. As children, we did not understand the financial devastation our family was experiencing due to the floods. We did not know the sorrow and hopeless fears of our parents as they saw everything destroyed for the second time in the same planting season. Hope for a crop was non-existent. There was fear of imminent financial collapse. The gnawing pain of sorrow and self-condemnation was relentless. Mental breakdown was highly probable.

As our crops were flooded and destroyed for the second time, my brother Dan and I, just little children, were having fun playing in the flood waters. Unbeknownst to me, my life as an innocent child was about to end. I do not remember what we did to cause our dad to snap, but he did, and he began to beat us with a piece of heavy-duty fueling hose. Danny took the first round of beatings, and I received the second round.

I could not understand why we were being beaten, but dad seemed to be out of his mind. He had become a different man; cursing me with every degrading word in his vocabulary. He beat me all over my head, back, buttocks, and legs until my body was numb and beyond experiencing pain.

I refused to cry, and that made dad even crazier with rage. He beat me even harder yelling, "You little S.O.B! You will either cry, or I will kill you!"

Though my body was numb beyond experiencing pain, as Dad continued to beat me and cuss me, my soul began to die within me. Finally, I whimpered like a beaten dog. I whimpered, not because of the bruised body but because I was losing my soul. I was losing my life as I had known it.

I was aware a transition was taking place, but I did not know how to stop it. My beautiful life of joy and peace was being removed and replaced with a life of deep darkness, full of hatred, pain, and vengeance. A devil entered me while I was whimpering and took me over from that very moment. I did not know how to resist the devil. He came in without my permission, and as I said, he did not leave until I was born again in May 1977.

To seal the deal, the devil branded my soul with the word coward. He called me a coward because I broke. You cannot imagine the torment that brand caused me all my life. It drove me to retaliate against all perceived resistance and confrontation.

A good friend of mine, Andre Barnum, and his wife Michelle could see this personality flaw in me and gave me a book entitled "Confrontation is Not Conflict." I knew they were right, so I tried to read it, but never finished it. I knew Andre and Michelle Barnum loved me. They were trying to bless me, but I chuckled at the title. I had no life experiences that related to the title of that book.

My dad raised us to know beyond a shadow of a doubt that his was the only acceptable opinion, and any dissenting opinion would be met with conflict, beating the opposition into submission. He trained us with these very words, "I do the thinking, and you do the doing."

He gave the orders, and we obeyed without hesitation. He called, and we came to attention. He commanded us, and we ran with all our might to carry out the command. He gave us further orders while we were running to accomplish the first orders, and we adjusted our course by his word. Nothing was done without conflict and stress. Conflict was normal. Peace was never a part of our life.

11

Even at seventy years of age, painful memories cry for my attention, and I must kill their influence by rehearsing the promises of God. I am fully aware that many children and wives have suffered much worse than our family, but our scars are our scars.

The scarring of the human soul is determined by (1) abuse to the body, (2) abuse to the hardwiring of personality types, (3) abuse to the gifts and callings of God in our lives, and (4) abuse to the imagination, desires, dreams, hopes and possibilities of having a better life.

From the time hell was beaten into me, I have always judged any challenge or disagreement as aggression and a call for war. I will elaborate for the sake of your understanding.

Individuals, like me, who fear conflict, are flawed with the drive to perform perfectly. We truly believe we have already worked out in our minds all the options and all the possibilities of failure and success. If our plan is challenged, we bristle.

Those of us with this kind of personality are truly flawed, believing it is our responsibility to never err. We are more than cautious to declare our plan of action for fear of being confronted. We truly believe we have considered all possibilities and are fully persuaded there could not be an alternative plan of action. Any suggestion of change is deemed conflict. We hate conflict, so we diligently labor to produce, not the best plan but the only sensible plan.

My original personality was very meek and mild. I did not start trouble, but I was not afraid to deal with any confrontation by words or physical force. At that time, confrontation was certainly not something I sought out, but I was comfortable dealing with it as it came to me. If I could restore that way of responding to conflict and confrontations, life would be much easier.

I traded a supernatural life of joy and peace for a devil-driven life of hatred, murder, and vengeance. Unwarranted murderous beatings severely bruised my spiritual connections. However, God remained faithful to me. He continued to supernaturally protect me

12

and keep me from committing murder or being murdered. Throughout my life, God has never left me. He has always been faithful in His commitment to keep me, to position me and to use me for His good. God has never abused me!

Many of us did not open the gates of hell and all the influences of darkness into our lives. Those who had authority over us opened the gates of hell, and all of us have suffered much needlessly.

Though dark in nature, many of the following life events have profound significance in my supernatural life. These events are recorded with the intent to show the goodness of God, even in the midst of the darkest times of our lives. Though devilish insanity began to rule the Craig's lives, God's Supernatural Deliverance was manifested many times.

Craziness in our society is more common than we desire to confess; especially when it happens within our families. If you have never met crazy, you have had a blessed but unusual life, at least unusual to me. The things that I will reveal about my family are crazy and true, but in no way mentioned to malign anyone. They are just the facts.

I might have become the craziest of all, especially in the darkest recesses of my soul. I spent much of my life planning vengeance and murder. I am glad I never succeeded. God has always been good to me, and through much longsuffering on His part, led me into a changed life in Christ.

At my salvation in May 1977, God delivered me from a murderous heart and taught me through Scriptures and many life experiences to obey the Love principle and live in peace. We certainly do not have complete control of other's aggression toward us, but we do have control of our response toward them.

The flesh usually cries for vengeance, as mine did, but vengeance becomes an addiction that can never be satisfied. Our heart cries for peace, but it never comes, as our minds remain blinded to the principles of Life. We struggle in our own willpower, never achieving peace and living a wasted life. All the pain caused

13

by darkness blinds us and delays us from fulfilling our God-given purpose. I am glad that God was longsuffering toward me and managed to save my very ugly soul.

> Numbers 14:18-21 (KJV)
> [18] The LORD is longsuffering, and of great mercy, forgiving iniquity and transgression, and by no means clearing the guilty, visiting the iniquity of the fathers upon the children unto the third and fourth generation. [19] Pardon, I beseech thee, the iniquity of this people according unto the greatness of thy mercy, and as thou hast forgiven this people, from Egypt even until now. [20] And the LORD said, I have pardoned according to thy word: [21] But as truly as I live, all the earth shall be filled with the glory of the LORD.

God has surely forgiven me, pardoned me, saved me and filled me with His glory. He desires to do the same for all of us.

# 4

# In the late 1950s: Preparation for a Pounding

Though my life of dreams and visions of what was happening in the kingdom of God were now very rare, I remained blessed to have an occasional vision that was to prepare me for something difficult coming into my life. At this young age, I was ignorant that

I had been called to the office of a Prophet and certainly no one I associated with would have confirmed it. As you now know, Prophets do not always see the lily white and all the glory of the light. Sometimes they see the pain and the sorrow and the darkness of the night.

As the prophet Ahijah was warned of things to come, I was also warned of things to come. He was warned of a coming liar, and I was warned of soon coming beating and pounding.

> 1 Kings 14:5-6 (KJV) 5 And the LORD said unto Ahijah, Behold, the wife of Jeroboam cometh to ask a thing of thee for her son; for he is sick: thus and thus shalt thou say unto her: for it shall be, when she cometh in, that she shall feign herself to be another woman. 6 And it was so, when Ahijah heard the sound of her feet, as she came in at the door, that he said, Come in, thou wife of Jeroboam; why feignest thou thyself to be another? for I am sent to thee with heavy tidings.

It was not uncommon for those of us struggling financially to use a battery beyond its useful life to start an engine. When this happened, and it often did, we pulled the tractor or vehicle with its transmission in gear. This caused the engine to turn over and start running. Though there was not enough electricity in the battery to start the engine, there was enough electricity to cause the spark plugs to send a spark into the engine cylinders to burn the fuel and keep the engine running.

On one fateful day, one of our M-Farmall tractors would not start, so big brother Bob and I engaged the above procedure to start the tractor's engine. I hooked it to another working M-Farmall tractor by a log-chain.

I must have inadvertently put the transmission in reverse rather than first gear, and while trying to start the tractor, a part broke in the starter or transmission. The sound of metal on metal was an alarm clock awakening my well-established fears of a coming beating. I did not know what broke, a bearing, a shaft, a tooth off the flywheel, a tooth off the starter. But as soon as the part broke, I had a vision of my dad coming from the field and beating us.

Within five minutes after the vision, while Bob and I were trying to solve the problem, my dad came from the field, just as I had seen in the vision. He was on the very tractor I had seen in the vision, taking the very route I had seen in the vision, and beat us exactly as I had seen in the vision.

The beating was unnecessary and not at all instructive, but I had no fear because I knew what the future held for me. Sometimes a supernatural warning comes to *prepare* us rather than to deliver us. Sometimes, to know your future eliminates fear.

The beating was brutal, but it did not bother me because I was prepared for it. I did not laugh out loud while I was being beaten, for that would have been more detrimental to my well-being, but I did grin on the inside because he was not able to terrorize me.

Fear causes torment, and sometimes laughter is a powerful antidote.

1 John 4:18 (KJV)
    [18] There is no fear in love; but perfect love casteth out fear: because fear hath torment. He that feareth is not made perfect in love.

Proverbs 17:22 (KJV)
    [22] A merry heart doeth good like a medicine: but a broken spirit drieth the bones.

Romans 10:17 (KJV)
  Faith cometh by hearing and hearing
by the word of God, Romans 10:17.

By hearing God through the vision, I had faith to face the future without fear. We can learn to use our faith to change a coming situation, but I did not know that at that time. That vision was enough to give me confidence that God was still working on my behalf. Without these supernatural dreams and visions, I believe I would have cracked in my mind or committed murder, hoping to be freed from the in-house terrorist, my dad.

# 5

# Late 1950s/early 1960s: Murder on the Basketball Court

Once darkness enters your life and is not immediately eradicated, it will take more ground and build greater strongholds in your soul to control your life. Darkness will not rely on your own sins to control you but will also use outside forces to destroy your hope for a better life. The devil used my big brother Bob to play this part on many occasions. The earliest recollection of Bob attacking my life was during a friendly game of basketball. He exploded into a rage and intended to kill me.

My death was imminent as Bob rammed the barrel of his twenty-gauge shot-gun up under my rib cage and into my diaphragm. I felt like 'twinkle toes,' being raised up as far as I could stretch on my tiptoes. The shotgun was loaded with a powerful long brass shell loaded with number six lead shot. If Bob had pulled the trigger, the lead would have blown a hole completely through my body cavity, and I would have fallen dead instantly. The hope of my life returning to a normal, peaceful life of living in the supernatural fellowship with God and his angels would have been over. Thank God I survived that day without harm and was extended more opportunities to try to return to the good life of living in the supernatural.

Though it is shocking, murder among siblings is not unheard of. The same sin that caused the first murder is still causing murders today. It is first mentioned in the Genesis account of mankind.

> Genesis 4:6-10 (KJV)
> "And the LORD said unto Cain, Why art thou wroth? and why is thy countenance fallen? 7 If thou doest well, shalt thou not be accepted? and <u>if thou doest not well, sin lieth at the door</u>. And unto thee shall be his desire, <u>and thou shalt rule over him</u>. 8 And Cain talked with Abel, his brother: and it came to pass, when they were in the field, that Cain rose up against Abel his brother, and slew him. 9 And the LORD said unto Cain, Where is Abel thy brother? And he said, I know not: Am I my brother's keeper? 10 And he said, What hast thou done? <u>the voice of thy brother's blood crieth unto me from the ground</u>."

If my memory serves me, I believe it was all of us Craig boys and some neighbors were playing basketball in the backyard. Our basketball court was bare, packed gumbo dirt, totally devoid of grass. We played there so often no grass could survive.

Something or someone, maybe even me, must have rubbed my older brother wrong. I might have called a foul when it was not, I might have used some cuss words, or I might have called him some degrading names. I don't remember. All of the above were forms of trash talk, and without coaches and referees, all is fair in love and war, and basketball in the backyard. Whatever or whomever caused the rub, the spirit of murder was loosed upon our basketball court. Bob lost his temper and lost control of his senses; enough that he went to get his shotgun to even the score.

I was very familiar with the gun as I had used it many times in hunting rabbits. It was single shot Champion shot-gun. I could see that he had the hammer back and his finger on the trigger. He was totally out of control, raging against me. I don't remember what he said to me, but after he calmed down, he released me. As he turned from me, he broke the barrel down and unloaded a long brass shell. I recognized that it was loaded with number six lead shot.

From my vantage point, the threat to kill me was very real. He was addressing me with all the cuss and venom within him. From the time the barrel of the shotgun was pushed into my abdomen, up under my rib cage, into my diaphragm, my emotions moved into neutral. It was a supernatural response initiated by God to protect me. I did nothing to protect myself. I did not try to talk him down, nor did I move a muscle to free myself from danger.

Typically, I would have tried to push the gun away from my belly or to take it from him and maybe even turn it on him. But if I had moved even the slightest amount in self-defense, by reflex, he would have pulled the trigger, and I would have been killed. Now, later in life, I have heard of others who have had their natural reasoning supernaturally suspended and taken over by God in order to protect them from being killed in the moment, by forces beyond their capacity to control. God was very good to all of us that day and stopped the killing.

That was not the only "confrontation/conflict" in our lives, but it was the only time he threated to kill me with a gun. Our angels were with us that day and defeated the spirit of murder. Angels had truly protected the Craig clan, and my supernatural life of dreams and visions continued.

Psalm 91:9-11 (KJV)

9 Because thou hast made the LORD, which is my refuge, even the most High, thy habitation; 10 There shall no evil befall thee, neither shall any plague come nigh thy dwelling. 11 For he shall give his angels charge over thee, to keep thee in all thy ways.

Never underestimate God's supernatural method of deliverance from death to keep us progressing forward to our gifts and callings. Paul first thought that God had called him for His will and purpose from his mother's womb, Galatians 1:15 but had a later revelation that God had called him even before the foundation of the world, Ephesians 1:4.

For some of you, you want to quit. You think God has abandoned you. I am writing my biography of these crazy events in my life to make you aware that even though the world seems to be completely against you, God is totally for you. *Please! Don't stop now!* I promise you; there are better days ahead.

To you, my life might appear to have been easy street. Many of you have suffered much more than me. My life could have been much worse, but to my personality, it was hell on earth.

God has not chosen that we suffer this hell but that we are delivered from all its evil intent, 2 Corinthians 1:8-11. The purpose of the devil's assaults on our lives is not just to kill us, but to get us to quit on God and fail to achieve our destiny in Christ Jesus.

Follow your dreams and visions that are from God and achieve what no person, other than God, believes you can achieve!

# 6

# 1963:
# Before School Let Out for Summer:
# A Terrifying Attack with a Knife

As you read, please keep in mind that I am relating these stories to you, not to malign my family, but to encourage you to pass through even greater trials than I have faced and become more successful than me. Every trial that I have shared and will share has had a devilish intent to stop God's voice from coming through me to bring a message of hope in Christ to a lost and dying world. That is the devil's same purpose for afflicting you.

Some of the prophets, both of The Old Testament and The New Testament suffered much. And the apostle Paul said he thought the apostles were the offscouring of the earth. Sometimes we are tormented from outside sources, and other times we are afflicted by those who should have honored us but either way, we continue to press toward the mark of the prize of the high calling of God in Christ Jesus.

In one of my dad's crazy rages and separations from sanity, he pushed his knife blade against my belly to stab me. Obviously, this should not be accepted as normal, corrective measures between parent and child.

At the time death is stalking us, we need some help from heaven. I got my help in a very supernatural way. God has been my great deliverer on many occasions.

Though crazy had become normal for us, some crazy was beyond any supposed acceptable limits. My maternal grandmother was dying, so my mom and her siblings had gathered in Trenton, Tennessee to be with their mother in her final moments.

Mom's absence put dad in stress. He had five children at home. He was also stressed after hearing that mom and most of her siblings had been cheated out of their inheritance. One of mom's siblings who had given grandma more physical attention changed the will to move the bulk of the inheritance to her account.

Grandma died, and a death certificate was signed, but after being in heaven for a short time, she returned to earth. She shared about her visit to heaven, her frustration of being back on earth and her desire to return to heaven. During the brief time she was alive for the second time, the daughter who deemed herself deserving her mother's inheritance, had a new will written. She brought in a shyster lawyer that helped change the will and leave the inheritance to her. Mom and all her siblings were cheated out of their inheritance. They were dealing with a double sorrow and did not fight their sister.

Meanwhile, back home in Essex Missouri, my older brother Bob and I were going on with life without trouble. Bob had his driver's license, and we had the family pickup truck at school. One of our friends, who was riding shotgun, opened the door and caught it on a post as the truck was moving in reverse. A lot of damage was done the door. We knew dad would explode when he saw the damage, but we were not prepared for the atomic blast that came from his broken soul. We had no idea of the trouble that lay before us.

When we came home and showed dad the damage, he exploded into a violent rage. He was crazier than a rabid dog. If ever there was time that he was totally consumed by devils, that surely must have been the time. He beat Bob severely with his fist, then threw him to the ground and continued to kick and stomp him with his boots. Bob was very badly bruised, cut and swollen, so I took him into the house to clean up his wounds. After dressing his wounds, we gathered ourselves and dressed to leave home to go out on our own. We probably had all of our earthly belongings in a brown paper grocery bag.

God had not told us to leave. We were just trying to survive and escape the terrorism in our family. Neither of us was afraid of work. We knew if anyone would hire us we could do a better job for them than any one of their laborers. When dad saw what we were doing, he grabbed me and slammed me into the corner of the kitchen cabinets.

He pulled his pocket knife on me and opened the three-inch blade on his Schrade-Walden pocket knife, pushing it to my navel. I could feel the tip of the blade. We were nose to nose. He had gotten close enough to me to have bitten off my nose. He cussed me with his most vehement cussing and called me an ungrateful little S.O.B., yelling that he should cut my guts out.

During all of his insane raging, threatening, and pushing the tip of his knife blade into my flesh, I had no fear of him or death. I would not dare call it love for him at that moment. I must have experienced a supernatural infusion of God's love, for fear could not torment me.

Again, the Holy Spirit made me go into neutral and not resist him. The Holy Ghost and angels did for me what they had done for me when Bob threatened to kill with his 20-gauge Champion, single-shot shotgun. My natural reasoning was again suspended by supernatural means, and I followed the course of my heart rather than the course of my flesh. After he began to calm down, he pulled back and folded his knife. If I had kicked him or hit him, he would have stabbed me by reflex, and my guts would have spilled out on our kitchen floor.

Through these demonic beatings to me and my siblings, my desire to kill him grew ever stronger. Through much meditation of murder and vengeance, I had some workable plans to take him out and cover it as a farm accident, but the Holy Ghost supernaturally prevented me from carrying out my plans. All this terror was killing my soul day by day, and a murderous heart was being formed with me.

Maybe my dreams turned from hearing the voice of God, to dreams to do His will, to becoming successful far away from this insanity, but God was able to keep my dream life alive. At this time, my dreams may have become more like fantasies. Maybe I was on cruise control, but I was still dreaming and moving forward. Our dreams become our blueprints or hope of change. I still have my blueprints. Keep your blueprints.

Fast forward to the last time of this kind of craziness. It was in 2006. Even at 86 years old he wanted to beat me again, and I finally had it out with him.

I brought up all his terroristic activities against his family. At first, he denied it and then said, "You should have killed me," to which I readily agreed, but I am glad I did not murder him.

There were many times I could have killed him and covered it up as a farm accident. I know if I had killed him, my life would have been a miserable, short, murderous life to hell.

God spared me!

# 7

# 1968:
# Murder in the Family

Sometimes I wonder if those of us who have this wonderful life of dreams and visions are not attacked more aggressively by the powers of darkness to remove us or our influence from the earth. The devil is a cagey creature. He moves our broken lives on the board of life like chess players move pawns on the table. The devil is always looking for 'checkmate,' but God is always showing us one more move!

By this time, my dreams were not so much for prediction of the future or any radical revelation, but to give me a hope that God had not abandoned me. Somehow, God was using these dreams to keep me connected to him and keeping me from taking vengeance upon my dad.

After my dad snapped and beat us, beatings became the daily pattern within the Craig clan. Dad took all his frustration out on his family. We were the only thing he was sure he could control. He could not control nature. He could not control the commodities market. He could not control the interest rates. He could not control his neighbors, but he could control us, and he did. He really thought he was in control, but truthfully, he was being controlled.

Gradually, the devil took control of all our lives! We exercised no control over our tempers, and we fought without mercy. It is truly the grace of God that prevented us from murdering one another. There were many times I wanted to override the witness in my spirit not to yield to murder, but God kept me. I did not know much about the Bible, church or the Christian life but by the grace of God, I had been given a conscience the first day I attended a church service, and my conscience has been my very good guide.

As I mentioned earlier, if the devil cannot trip you and stop you by your own sin, he will use an outside force and finally, murder found an entry into our family. It never loosed its grip on us until we were born again Christians. It came in through my brother-in-law, Dave. He may have picked up that murderous spirit by marrying into our family, but I don't know.

Dave and my sister Jeanice had been married about five years. They were terminating their marriage, but he killed her and later himself on the day they were to be divorced.

We do not know the reason they were together that day, as they had separate residences. Dave might have been trying to persuade

Jeanice not to go through with the divorce. In the very early morning, before sunrise, just hours before Jeanice was to report to her job as a teacher, they were both dead. Our family, as well as his, would never be the same.

Apparently, he had shared with his friends that if the divorce was finalized, he would commit suicide. He even showed them the place he had chosen to end his life. No one thought he was serious about his threats. They suspected it was a method of manipulating his wife to try to work things out in the marriage. Though not for the same reasons as he had stated, he did kill himself.

He killed himself by driving her car at maximum speed, 120 mph +, into the flood wall of the Mississippi River in Granite City, Illinois.

Apparently, he was accurate in his approach to the wall, and the car body crushed and folded in like the material of a handheld accordion. His body and the body of the car became one. The wreckage was removed to a local garage where his body was cut out in parts. His body parts were shipped to his family. None of our family attended his funeral.

My brother-in-law had been frustrated with his life. He had struggled with submission to his dad but idolized my dad's very worst trait, control. Dave was a very capable man, but he was very dissatisfied with his achievements. Like my dad, he could not control life around him, so he began to control what he could, his wife. He idolized the control my dad's anger had over his family, so he put that into practice in his own family. Dave's anger, though probably not nearly as crazy as my dad's anger, bore the fruit of the one driving him, murder.

Proverbs 22:24-25 (KJV)
24 Make no friendship with an angry man; and with a furious man, thou shalt not go:
25 Lest thou learn his ways and get a snare to thy soul.

John 8:44 (KJV)

⁴⁴ Ye are of your father the devil, and the lusts of your father ye will do. He was a murderer from the beginning, and abode not in the truth because there is no truth in him. When he speaketh a lie, he speaketh of his own: for he is a liar and the father of it.

My mother never rose above the pain and sorrow of my sister's murder. Mom wanted an answer to her daughter's murder and never stopped asking the question, *"Why?"* Dad said that often in the middle of the night, unconscious of her actions, mom would be pounding on him screaming, *"Why?!"* Not many months before her death, I sat with her in the south living room of her house, listening to her question why. She never got her answer, or she never obeyed the command to forgive. Mom died prematurely at age sixty-seven of a broken heart.

Though Dad claimed he never had dreams, and I know of only one vision he shared with me, he could understand the written Word of God and would obey it in the crucial times of his life. None of the rest of us followed that part of his life. We became even more fragmented and drawn away from the supernatural life into a more carnal life away from the will and call of God on our lives.

My dad, crazy as he was, had knowledge of the Bible and took hold of a Scripture that saved his life.

Matthew 6:19-21 (KJV)

¹⁹ Lay not up for yourselves treasures upon earth, where moth and rust doth corrupt, and where thieves break through and steal: ²⁰ But lay up for yourselves treasures in heaven, where neither moth nor rust doth corrupt, and where thieves do not

break through nor steal: 21 For where your treasure is, there will your heart be also.

Dad was very explosive in his anger. He would be white hot in a flash. His terrible eruptions of explosive insanity seemed to be a pressure relief valve for him. His explosions left shrapnel in everyone around him, but he was freed. After he calmed down, he seldom looked back. He seldom held on to his bitterness. It was a supernatural work of God in his life to forgive and go forward for himself. However, he left the rest of us in shambles.

Matthew 5:43-48 (KJV)
43 Ye have heard that it hath been said, Thou shalt love thy neighbour, and hate thine enemy. 44 But I say unto you, Love your enemies, bless them that curse you, do good to them that hate you, and pray for them which despitefully use you, and persecute you; 45 That ye may be the children of your Father which is in heaven: for he maketh his sun to rise on the evil and on the good, and sendeth rain on the just and on the unjust. 46 For if ye love them which love you, what reward have ye? do not even the publicans the same? 47 And if ye salute your brethren only, what do ye more than others? Do not even the publicans so? 48 Be ye therefore perfect, even as your Father which is in heaven is perfect.

Forgive and live to be of a ripe, old age, full of days, full of riches and full of honor. Dad had experienced some very painful things during WWII. Maybe that is why he had to lean on scriptures to survive and overcome those memories. God honors us where we honor His Word. Dad honored God's Word in forgiveness and lived to seventeen days short of ninety. Mom did not forgive and died at the age of sixty-seven.

The spirit of murder kills from the outside and the inside. It is much like General Sherman's march to the sea; it will destroy everything in its path. These tragedies continued to fragment our lives and destroy our hope for a better future. My supernatural life of dreams and visions had lost all of its luster, but was still used to save my life and keep me from taking vengeance. All supernatural events are not spectacular, and all spectacular events are not supernatural. I favor the supernatural in my life. It has been very good to me.

# 8

# 1968 April:
# Threatened with a 45 Caliber MDL 1911 Pistol

Sometimes in my life, I felt like someone had hired the old soldier of fortune, 'Paladin, Have Gun Will Travel' to kill me. This time the would-be killer met me in Batesville, Mississippi, just a few miles from my dormitory on the campus of Ole Miss, University of Mississippi. I was threatened with a pistol by a local citizen, and again, God was faithful to deliver from death. I was age twenty and in my junior year at the University of Mississippi, Ole Miss, Oxford, Mississippi. I had gone to the county line, West of Batesville MS, with some friends to drink and party. In Lafayette County, where we lived, beer could not be sold to anyone less than 21 years of age.

29

On the way home, we irritated a local citizen by beating him in a friendly road race. We were in a 1956 Chevrolet that had been modified with a 1963 Corvette motor and drive train. Our contender was driving a new Chevrolet and was humiliated for his loss.

Our driver, Albert, pulled over in Batesville to finish the challenge with a fist fight. When we stopped in a very large parking lot, the loser in the race pulled up beside us. I looked to my right, intending to get out and help Albert, if necessary and quickly realized I was facing an angry man who was holding his 45-caliber pistol, model 1911. He pointed it toward me, as I was against the passenger door and began to cuss me and threaten me while accenting his words, jabbing and waving his pistol towards me. The muzzle of the pistol was within three feet of me, and if he had pulled the trigger, I would have been severely wounded, if not killed.

Albert did not see the pistol until he had walked around beyond the right front fender of our car. He pulled himself up short and hesitated until he could discern the situation. Sometimes, when alcohol impaired my better judgment, I would retaliate when it was not in my best interest. Again, God put me in neutral, and the enraged man gradually calmed down and withdrew his pistol.

I do not know if you have ever had one of these supernatural anointings where you are supernaturally directed by the Holy Ghost. In the natural, it appeared as if Albert talked him down, but I know differently. By this time in my life, my sensitivity to the unction of the Holy Ghost and my inward witness was significantly dulled, but God was so merciful to me to keep me alive. Sin, hatred, vengeance and a murderous heart were setting me up for a sure death. By God's mercy, we made our way back to Oxford, to our dormitories, glad to be alive, and the contender went on his way considering himself the victor.

Angels were unquestionably protecting us. Surely, Christians were or had been in prayer for me during these threats of murder! Maybe God was answering prayers of the saints who were praying in the Holy Ghost. It has never been revealed to me why God protected me, but I know that I did not protect myself. Surely, angels, who are ministering spirits for us who shall be the heirs of salvation, were keeping their assignment in my life.

> 2 Kings 19:35-36 (KJV)
> 35 And it came to pass that night, that the angel of the LORD went out, and smote in the camp of the Assyrians an hundred fourscore and five thousand: and when they arose early in the morning, behold, they were all dead corpses. 36 So Sennacherib king of Assyria departed, and went and returned, and dwelt at Nineveh.

# 9

# 1971 May: The Angry Neighbor

Have you ever questioned the possibility you were wearing a sign saying, ATTACK ME! I felt like the devil had posted my wanted poster in the sky. This particular crazy incident was caused by my own foolishness. It was in the spring of 1971, in Jonesboro, Arkansas that a man threatened to beat me because he accused me of shooting his house.

I had been using my Savage, 12-gauge, semi-automatic shotgun to shoot some blackbirds. I admitted I had shot in the general direction of his house but argued it was such a distance that the light load number 8 shot could not have reached his property. None the less, he was not properly impressed and came charging me, expressing his dislike, cussing me and threatening me with bodily harm. Since hell was beaten into me at ten years of age, and I had lost my peaceful soul, for the next twenty years it seemed I was a magnet for raging lunatics desiring to kill me!

When he was within twenty-five feet of me, I raised the shotgun toward his chest. I threatened to kill him, and when he looked down the barrel of the twelve-gauge Savage Shotgun, he came up short, paused and backed down. We parted company without harming one another.

The supernatural blessing was that as he came charging me, I had unconsciously unloaded my gun of all ammunition and put the shells into my pocket. I credit God with that decision because when he charged, and I raised the gun to kill him, I did not remember I had unloaded the shot-gun. If it had been loaded and I had pulled the trigger, I would have been a murderer. If I had pulled the trigger and he realized the gun was empty of ammunition, he might have taken the gun from me and beaten me to death, and he would have been the murderer. It was not until after I had been saved for a few years that I began to realize how many times God spared my life from killing or being killed.

# *10*

# On July 11, 1971:
# From Stone Dead to Life

Some Christians, even ministers, do not believe people can be raised back to natural life after they have died, but I was raised from a true death, not near death, after drowning.

Jesus raised people from the dead. Jesus' disciples raised people from the dead. Christians can raise people from the dead. Even EMTs and doctors can bring people back from the dead.

Luke 7:12-15 (KJV)

12 Now when he came nigh to the gate of the city, behold, there was <u>a dead man carried out</u>, the only son of his mother, and she was a widow: and much people of the city was with her. 13 And when the Lord saw her, he had compassion on her, and said unto her, Weep not. 14 And he came and touched the bier: and they that bare him stood still. And he said, <u>Young man, I say unto thee</u>, <u>Arise</u>. 15 And <u>he</u> <u>that was dead sat up</u> <u>and began to speak</u>. And he delivered him to his mother.

Acts 9:36-41King James Version (KJV)

36 Now there was at Joppa a certain disciple named Tabitha, which by interpretation is called Dorcas: this woman was full of good works and alms deeds which she did.37 And it came to pass in those days, that she was <u>sick</u>, and <u>died</u>: whom when they had washed, they laid her in an upper chamber. 38 And forasmuch as Lydda was nigh to Joppa, and the disciples had heard that Peter was there, they sent unto him two men, desiring him that he would not delay to come to them. 39 Then Peter arose and went with them. When he was come, they brought him into the upper chamber: and all the widows stood by him weeping, and shewing the coats and garments which Dorcas made, while she

was with them. [40] But <u>Peter</u> put them all forth, and kneeled down, and prayed; and turning him to the body <u>said, Tabitha, arise</u>. And <u>she opened her eyes</u>: and when she saw Peter, <u>she sat up</u>. [41] And he gave her his hand and lifted her up, and when he had called the saints and widows, <u>presented her alive.</u>

During the summer of 1971, I was being trained by the United States Army at Fort Riley Kansas. At the conclusion of the camp, I was to be commissioned as an officer, 2nd Lieutenant, in the US Army, Medical Service Corp.

On the fateful Sunday morning, July 11, 1971, I had a warning from God to not do anything stupid and to stay out of sin that day. Stupid and sin are both broad terms, but I knew enough to understand; trouble was stalking me.

However, some friends in the barracks first encouraged me and then convinced me to buy some beer and go to Milford Lake to swim. That should have been warning enough because I am a poor swimmer. I swim poorly enough in an Olympic size pool but even worse in a river or lake. My confidence is tremendously improved if I can see the depth of the water.

We purchased some 3.2 % beer and went to swim in Milford Lake, which is nearby Fort Riley. I swam out to some buoys around a designated swimming area and decided to rest before returning to shore. I needed to rest because I do not know how to properly take a breath when I am swimming. Because of this, my distance is limited, and I need to stop, rest and to take another breath. The buoys were spinning around the connecting cable and were slick from algae, so I let go to swim back to shore.

Immediately after releasing from the buoys, fear gripped me, and my muscles cramped and knotted so I could no longer swim. I was thrashing in the water but was not moving forward. I began to cry for help, but my friends must have thought I was just goofing around. They did not leave the shore to rescue me. I went under water and ingested some water into my lungs on the way to the surface. My lungs filling with water released more fear and assured me of my doom.

I knew I was dying. I was screaming bloody murder. I was cussing my friends for not coming to my rescue. I went down the second time and took in more water. I became even more fearful of dying. Before I went down the third time, I had this cruel thought come to my mind! If I go down the third time, I will surely drown. I went down for the third time. I saw the red water close over my face as I was sinking. I did surely drown.

Immediately, I was out of my body, and my spirit was up in the sky looking at my body suspended just a few feet under the surface. The body was floating somewhat like a jelly-fish. I examined the body, but I had no desire for it. My spirit was suspended some distance above ground, maybe one hundred yards. I took the time to look around, and everything was beautiful. The colors of vegetation, rocks, and the sky were all more beautiful than I can describe.

I was suspended and not moving. I was not in a tunnel moving toward light or darkness. Everything was beautiful, and I was at total peace. Though I was dead and separated from my body, I had no fear of being separated from it and had no desire for it.

As I was surveying the beautiful surroundings, my attention was drawn to a fluffy cloud that was moving toward me. I became interested in the cloud and began to move toward the cloud.

Without moving my limbs to walk toward the cloud, I entered into it. I do not remember making a conscious decision to enter the cloud nor to leave the cloud. The cloud totally encompassed me. I could not see anything or anyone inside the cloud. The cloud seemed to be a warm light. It was like light coming from and incandescent light bulb.

Shortly after entering the cloud I began to hear voices; maybe many voices. I was not troubled by not being able to understand the voices. Now I would describe the voices as a Holy Ghost baptized believers' prayer meeting. Everyone was speaking at the same time.

Everything inside the cloud seemed pleasant and peaceful to me. Peace is the goal of my life and maybe the thing I long above everything else to experience in heaven.

Without making a personal decision to change position, I began to depart the cloud without moving a limb. I seemed to be moving on a flat conveyor belt. I do not know the amount of time I was inside the cloud. When I was outside the cloud, I saw a man pulling my body through the water.

As I observed a man pulling my dead body through the water, I began to move toward the body, without moving a limb. As I came closer to the body, I began a dive, similar to a super-man dive. I entered the body before the rescuer got my body to the shore. I later awakened lying on my back. One of my friend's faces was a few inches above my face and to my right side. My chest felt bruised and very sore. He had been doing life-saving techniques.

I stood up and the three of us, the two friends that had convinced me to come to the lake, and me, walked off down the beach.

Immediately upon regaining my consciousness inside my body, I began to see flashes of being outside my body. I remembered the arm's length distance from the right side of my face before my spirit re-entered my body. Because of the flashbacks, I don't remember our conversation while walking down the beach, nor do I remember our trip back to Fort Riley.

None of us ever discussed what happened that day. I disobeyed the warning and did something stupid. I *died* because of my disobedience, but by the grace of God, I was allowed to live again. Surely it was the prayers of the saints that moved God to save me. It was probably the saints' prayers I was hearing while inside the cloud. If not, I do not know who else to thank, except God Himself. I have recorded it as I remember it.

# *11*

# August 1971:
# An Intimidating Threat
# from the Devil

In early August, I was commissioned as a 2nd Lieutenant on the Parade Field of Fort Riley, Kansas. I married on August 14, 1971. During our honeymoon, I crossed the dam of Norfolk Lake, Arkansas and decided to stop and look over the rail down to the lake side of the water. As I was looking down at the lake, a voice spoke to me very clearly, *Jump! Prove to yourself you can swim.* It seemed like the one speaking was standing beside me. The memories of the drowning began to flood my soul. Without explaining anything to Harriet, I rushed into the car and quickly drove across the dam to the other side.

Later that day, I told her about my death by drowning and what was spoken to me while on the dam. She became very worried and said to me, "Never tell anyone what you just told me or they, the keepers of the asylum, will come carry you away in a little white suit."

I did not share the story again until 1980, three years after I had become a born-again Christian. I did not understand the event until 1980. At the time I was teaching a Bible study in Conquering Faith Center, Sikeston, Missouri. During the teaching, I quoted a testimony of a death experience of Kenneth E. Hagin, and suddenly, all the events of my death by drowning came back to me.

I had suppressed the memory of the drowning for nine years. After that night, I began to share it on a limited basis with some I thought might understand it. Once, I shared it with a friend, L. B.

Black of Essex, Missouri, and when I finished, L. B. looked straight at me and said, "Doc, I don't believe a thing you said," and he walked away.

Many years later, L. B. suffered a very severe stroke and had a similar experience as mine. He said, "Doc, I did not believe your story, but now I know it is true." He shared how he was out of his body and watched the doctors working feverishly to bring him back from death. He lived for a few more years.

If a person has never experienced death, they may refer to these as near-death experiences, but if you have ever died and been allowed to live again, you know you have experienced a true death with the spirit being absent from the body. As soon as your inward man leaves your body, you are dead. This is supported by Scripture.

James 2:26 (KJV)
26 For as the body without the spirit is dead, so faith without works is dead also.

2 Corinthians 5:6-8 (KJV)
6 Therefore we are always confident, knowing that, whilst we are at home in the body, we are absent from the Lord: 7 (For we walk by faith, not by sight:) 8 We are confident, I say, and willing rather to be absent from the body, and to be present with the Lord.

The first time I died, I died in complete terror. I hope to die in faith the next time with great joy, looking forward to achieving peace in a place where all tears are wiped away. Hopefully I will be like Paul and will say, I am ready to be offered up. I have fought the good fight. I have finished my course. I have kept the faith. Hopefully I will be allowed to complete much more of my course assignment before my departure.

# 12

# 1977 May:
# Saved at Last

We were married in August 1971 but only attended church a few times in the first three years of our marriage. In late 1974, I was honorably discharged from the Army and returned to live in Essex, Missouri. My wife Harriet decided to begin attending church again on a regular basis.

At an early age, Harriet had been raised in the Amboy United Methodist Church, North Little Rock, Arkansas. She had been confirmed by the time she was a teenager but had not attended church after we were married. She had been out of church for about four years; one in college and three with me.

Harriet and I met in college, Arkansas State University, Jonesboro, Arkansas. From the time we began to date, January 1971 until 1974, we had attended very few church services, but she was in a place she needed to return to her roots in Christianity. When we moved to Essex, a United Methodist Church was located just two blocks from our home. She returned to church and was enjoying her renewed commitment to God. After she was feeling better about her spiritual life, she began witnessing to me. Her witnessing made me extremely angry. I was adamantly opposed to hearing anything about the church or my need for salvation.

During my earlier years, maybe even some during my college years, I attended a General Baptist Church. I came away with the wrong impression, that if I could not stop sinning on my own, I could not be saved and would go to hell. They had me convinced, but after trying several times to stop sinning in my own strength, I failed. I gave up trying and accepted that my fate was an eternal hell. I am glad I was mistaken and could be saved.

I did not realize Harriet had shared some of her needs with other women and people were praying for her and praying for my salvation. Sometime early in 1975, I began to feel uncomfortable about my life. Their prayers were causing me to do some introspection. At first, I did not recognize that it was God messing with me. I thought the pressure from farming and the disappointment of not buying land was causing me to break down. But after more than a year I began to suspect God was trying to talk to me. The conviction lasted about two and a half years before I was saved. In late 1976 or early 1977, I had become convinced it was God talking to me, but I did not know how to respond to him. I never shared my pain, disappointment, and failures with anyone. I figured it was mine to deal with, and if it was to be solved, I could do it.

By March 1977, I was fully aware that God was calling me to an altar experience, but I was resisting it for two reasons: (1) I knew I would cry at the altar, and I did not want to break in front of anyone. (2) Many of the men in the church were local businessmen, and I did not want to show weakness in front of them. Though truthfully, when alone I had wept much through my life when talking to God. Many times, I would look up into the starry heavens and simply say in a child-like way, "God, come have a sodie with me." I had forgotten those simple prayers, but I now understand God was answering them and was trying to set a "sodie date."

I truly misunderstood salvation, thinking that I would be perceived as one who was weak and could not take the pressures of life. My brother Danny had been saved in 1975 and would ask me to attend special services with him among the Full Gospel Business Men meetings. I went on occasion but was set like flint not to go to the altar. I continued to attend church occasionally with Harriet, and the conviction was steadily building up within my heart.

On one occasion while we were singing the hymn "How Great Thou Art" I broke. I began to cry but caught myself and said under my breath, "Get out and leave me alone." He did! His presence was so absent that it scared me. I felt as if I was all alone in a glass room made of one-way mirrors. I could see the people on the outside. They would come to the mirror to adjust their clothing or comb their hair but could not see me.

I knew I had fouled up and said back, "God, I did not mean that, but I am not going to that altar."

He answered in a sharp authoritative voice, "If you do not go to that altar, you never will."

I argued my case with Him about my fears of breaking and crying, but He said nothing else about it. The convicting power of God continued to apply pressure on me to decide for salvation. I finally did what I had wanted to do for twenty years. I yielded that day in May of 1977 and became a Christian.

I went to church that day for the specific purpose of being saved. I shared my heart with my Sunday School Teacher, James Ross. He told me not to let the Devil steal another day from me, but I did not understand his message. I almost left the church at the end of the service without being saved.

That morning, for worship service, I sat near the front, rather than in the far back corner. I was so ready to be saved. I began to cry in one of the opening songs. The pastor did not know what to do with me and did not take advantage of my obvious brokenness. By the end of the service, I was ready to go home and go to work on the farm, but my wife Harriet came to my right side and placed her left arm through my right arm and just smiled. If she had said anything about going to the altar, I would have left the church. The devil will use anything to stop our salvation.

As Harriet was standing to my right, with her left arm through my right arm, I cried out **"What the hell, why not!"** and was saved. I know that is not a polished prayer, but it was very effective and effectual in my life. I was gloriously saved standing between the first

41

and second pew on the south side of the aisle in the First United Methodist Church, Essex, Missouri.

I have always been grateful that the members of that church allowed me to attend services with them. I was *rough!* I cussed terribly, even in the church.

After I was saved, I went forward and kneeled at the altar rail. Harriet kneeled on one side, and a good friend, Pat, knelt on the other side. Pat hugged me and said, "Honey, it is all over with now." That was a good prophecy. It stuck!

# *13*

# 1977 July: Water Baptized in a Swimming Pool

The Methodist Church baptized by sprinkling or by immersion as the candidate chose, and I chose to be immersed. Some friends, Taylor Brothers Farm, from whom I rented my house, had a swimming pool they allowed churches to use for water baptisms. I was water baptized in their swimming pool. I did not inform anyone in my natural family about the baptism. Harriet thought I should invite them, but I thought that none of them cared, so I kept quiet. Harriet or someone must have informed Dad of the date and time because when I came up out of the water, I saw him outside the pool area removing his glasses and wiping tears from his eyes.

My dad was saved later that year or in early 1978. I do not remember where he was water baptized. He soon became baptized with the Holy Ghost and was speaking in other tongues. He bore fruit according to Acts 1:8 and became a strong witness to his friends about his life change and the baptism with the Holy Ghost. His faith was growing, and he became excited about going to Tulsa Oklahoma in July 1978 to a Kenneth E. Hagin Camp meeting. He invited some very close friends of our family, Lee and Dorothy Bloomfield to go with us. He made some very real-life changes for good. Dad moved from a broken heart to a new creature in Christ Jesus.

God had exploded within the Craig family, and we were spreading the good news among our friends and anyone who would give us an ear. Holy Ghost meetings were popping up all around us, and we attended as many as we possibly could. The vision given to my brother Danny on the very night of his salvation that all the Craigs would be saved was coming to pass, and we were not quiet about it. Because of our crazy, hot-tempered, yelling cussing lifestyle, one of our neighbors had said about us, "If the Craigs can get saved, anyone can get saved," and she was correct! Crazy or not, when we turned to God with all of our hearts, He welcomed us with salvation without hesitation, and He will do the same for you.

# 14

# 1977 August:
# Holy Ghost Baptisms
# and Counter Attacks of Devils

As a young boy, we had friends that were Pentecostal, but we were not Christians. Wanda Steele and Jewel Lawrence were members of Assembly of God churches. Some people that lived on the farm were also Pentecostals, so we were familiar with speaking in tongues. One of the ladies on the farm would hide her self away in an old smokehouse to pray in other tongues. We would look through the cracks in the wall to listen and see what she was doing. I listened out of curiosity, but it had a profound effect on me.

As I continued my schooling, even through college, I associated with people who were Pentecostal. We never discussed their commitment to God nor the practices of their churches, especially speaking in other tongues. Some of the Pentecostal girls dressed rather plainly and did not party but were generally kind. About 25 percent of the members of the church in which I was saved were Charismatics. I paid attention to their testimonies of what the Holy Ghost was doing in their lives, and it caught my attention. I decided to be baptized with the Holy Spirit.

I had only been saved a few months and was ignorant of the Christian life, but I truly desired to baptized with the Holy Ghost and speak with other tongues.

The night we were going to the meeting, I was nervous. I fully expected the believers to pray for me to be baptized with the Holy Ghost, but I had no understanding of speaking in other tongues. We were stepping further into our supernatural life, not knowing we were stirring powers of darkness to counter-attack us.

On our car-port, my four-year-old son Matthew asked me a question as we were loading into the car. Just before we closed the doors, he said, "Dad, do you hear the wolves?"

I was a little taken aback but did make an effort to hear. I answered, "No, Matthew, I do not hear the wolves."

When were about half-way to the meeting, Matthew asked the same question, "Dad, do you hear the wolves?"

Again, I made a conscious effort to try to hear. I did not hear them, and I answered him again, "No, Matthew, I do not hear the wolves."

When we arrived at the meeting, I was even more excited about receiving the baptism with the Holy Ghost, and as I opened my car door and stepped out, I heard the sound of wolves just as though they were on the passenger side of the car. It made my hair stand on end! We did not realize the powers of darkness were *stalking us!*

I had no idea what was about to happen to our family. During the meeting, some spiritual confusion arose as the group was going to pray for an unsaved friend to baptized with the Holy Ghost. Unsaved people cannot be baptized with the Holy Ghost and newly saved people, as I was at that time, seem to be very sensitive to who is and who is not saved. Many people are members of churches but not citizens of the kingdom of God. I am not being critical, and discernment has nothing to do with the way they live, but the witness of the inward man makes the distinction.

During the confusion, I rounded up my family to leave, and as we were going out the door, Harry Glenn Williamson yelled out, "David, don't leave! You are the one that is to be baptized with the Holy Ghost." I answered yes and continued to proceed to the car, but Harry convinced me to come back for prayer. It was a beautiful experience to have a bunch of Charismatics pray for you to receive the baptism with the Holy Ghost with the evidence of speaking in other tongues.

Every person was giving different directions at the same time. Hold on. Let go. Say this. Lift your hands. Say whatever you hear in your spirit. Say this after me to prime your pump. They laid their hands on my head. They patted me on the back or head while praying in other tongues themselves. It was a glorious experience because they desired to see me experience the same blessing that had received. I do not know how much of the instruction was scriptural, but it was all done in love. This Holy Ghost baptized saint will always be grateful to them for their love for me. They were determined to see me receive the Promise of The Father.

The last instruction that I received was from Mrs. Helen Ross. "David, trust God. Whatever word or words you spoke are from God. Just as a baby practices repeating his limited vocabulary, you do the same, and the language will grow."

I obeyed her word of encouragement. I did speak a couple of words but did not repeat them in front of the people. Under my breath, I practiced with my two words as we returned home. When we arrived home, I immediately went into the house without helping Harriet with the children. She finished putting up things and came into the bedroom. She said I was stretched across the bed speaking in tongues. She shook me to consciousness to share the joy of what she heard, but I denied doing so because I did not hear myself. I could have been in a Holy Ghost trance.

I obeyed Mrs. Ross and practiced speaking my few words every day. One day, while marking for aerial application of fertilizer on rice, I was repeating the same phrases over and over again. I must have gone into a trance while repeating the few words of other tongues I had received at the prayer meeting. I came out of the trance as I heard the roar of the airplane's engine and felt the pellets of fertilizer hitting me in the face. Since that day I have had a very fluent flow of various languages of tongues.

Though I was growing in my confidence of speaking in other tongues, I usually spoke in tongues when no one was around me. On a day I had retired to my bedroom to pray in other tongues, Matthew opened the door and came in to check it all out. I stopped praying as he was coming around to face me from the other side of the bed. He put his elbows on the bed and his face in his hands and blessed me saying, "Dad, go ahead. I like it." That was a very blessed day for me! It freed me to speak in tongues with other believers during our prayer meetings.

Christians who are not praying in other tongues are missing out on the second most important supernatural thing in their life. Becoming a new creature in Christ Jesus is without exception the greatest supernatural act of God that will ever be done for a person. The third greatest supernatural act will be the resurrection from the dead into an immortal body. The first and the third are so magnificent that the second is often overlooked as unnecessary for today. Praying in other tongues is a supernatural gift from God.

Praying in other tongues is necessary to live the fullest Christian life. It increases our sensitivity to the witness of the Holy Spirit to our spirit. All Christians should obey Jesus and receive the promise of the Father, the baptism with the Holy Ghost, with the evidence of speaking in tongues.

> Acts 1:4-5, 8 (KJV)
> 4 And, being assembled together with them, commanded them that they should not depart from Jerusalem, but wait for the promise of the Father, which, saith he, ye have heard of me. 5 For John truly baptized with water; but ye shall be baptized with the Holy Ghost not many days hence. 8 But ye shall receive power, after that the Holy Ghost is come upon you: and ye shall be witnesses unto me both in Jerusalem, and in all Judaea, and in Samaria, and unto the uttermost part of the earth.

# *15*

# 1977 August:
# Demonic Outbreak in the House

From the night I was baptized with the Holy Ghost and began to speak in other tongues, we noticed demonic activity coming against us. The children, especially Matthew, began to have terrifying dreams of wolves coming into his room, and Harriet and I could sense a demonic presence and saw creatures moving through the house. As our Holy Ghost spiritual activity increased, the spiritual activity of darkness increased right along with our Holy Ghost development.

Sometimes, these creatures would move physical objects. Doors would open and slam closed. Dishes would move and rattle in the cabinets. Some creatures even appeared as physical beings.

Harriet was more discerning than me, but we both witnessed creatures in the house. We were afraid to share any of this with friends, so we sought instruction from books. We needed to purge our lives from these influences.

We purchased books from authors considered experts in purging houses of these creatures. We practiced their instruction to no avail. A popular book at that time was "Pigs in the Parlor" by Ida Mae Hammond. We read it and followed its instruction. It had no positive effect. The works of darkness increased. We burned everything we were instructed to burn, renounced and denounced any and everything that we thought may have opened the door to this demonic activity. Nothing changed!

We burned LP records we had purchased, gifts, anything on the hit list, but nothing improved. A friend named Al and his wife Diane had given me some small do-dads of owls. Owls were on the hit list according to the book "Pigs in the Parlor." I burned the wooden owl figurine in the outside trash burning pit. I was hoping that would be the end, but it was not. The next morning, I went out with the morning trash. That wooden owl figurine was standing on my back porch. I had personally thrown it into the burning fire, but here it stood with no damage, not even smoke damage.

Much more craziness happened than I have recorded. But this is sufficient to give you the picture of what was happening in our home. A powerful, supernatural darkness had a door into our lives, but we could not identify the door. We did not associate the time of its entrance with the night that I was baptized with the Holy Ghost and began to speak in other tongues.

Mark 16:17 (KJV)

<sup>17</sup> And these signs shall follow them that believe; <u>In my name</u> <u>shall they cast out devils</u>; they shall speak with new tongues;

Finally, we shared our dilemma with a very close friend, Vic McClung. He declared he was not afraid of anything and would come to our home and we would clean house of all this demonic activity. We had scriptural evidence to cast out devils, and we tried to apply it to our house.

Vic came, and we prayed, but we did not affect the darkness at all. At one point, while he sat on the sofa, he asked me what had come to stand beside him. I could tell a creature was standing beside him but could not describe it. At one-time Vic had worked in an ice house and described the creature as being as cold as a hundred-pound block of ice. We ended the prayer session in defeat, and he returned to his home.

Later Vic revealed that some of the spirits that were in my house departed with him. He felt like they departed before he returned to his home in Sikeston, Missouri.

After reading and practicing the instruction of many Pentecostal authors, including Kenneth E Hagin, T. L. Osborn, Lester Sumrall and many others, we gave up. You know the old phrase--*If you can't beat them, join them*--Well, we did *not* join them. However, we decided that since they were not leaving, and we had no other place to go, we would try to coexist. That was a mistake. Any time you yield territory to demons, they will gladly occupy it and take more. The devil is not a person of peace nor will he allow any Christian to experience peace if he has the slightest foothold in your life. Trying to coexist with him is like trying to coexist with a bad roommate in college. Eventually, one of the roommates will seek another residence. We liked our residence and did not want to seek another. We had rented the house, and the demons were squatters. They had

49

to go! But who was going to evict them? They were not moved by our Holy Ghost eviction notice.

On another occasion of visiting in Vic's home, another mutual friend, Freddy Phillips, was visiting at the same time. After a good visit, our family was proceeding out the back door to the car, but Freddy stopped me. He asked, "Are you having some demonic activity in your home?" I cut my eyes toward Vic to see if he had said anything to Freddy. He shook his head signaling he had not shared any of what we had shared with him. I was certainly ready to leave and not discuss anything about demons in my home, but Freddy was persistent! I showed some patience, though I did not believe a thing he was sharing with me. Freddy was questioning me about social, political, and religious organizations I had affiliated with, but he centered upon one, the Masonic Lodge.

Everything he was sharing was so bizarre to me; even more bizarre than having demons manifesting their presence in my home. He was telling me to renounce my association with the Masonic Lodge. I was friends with those lodge members. I attended church with some of them. I explained that what he was sharing was crazy. The whole conversation was very irritating to me. I had been a member of the Masonic Lodge for several years. I had never heard any of the members complaining about demonic activity in their house.

I was determined to leave, but Harriet was worn out from this spiritual activity. She was beginning to cry softly. Because of Harriet, I decided I would go along with it, but I did not believe a thing I had agreed to do. Freddy and I knelt in prayer in front of the McClung's sofa to renounce any association with the Masonic organization. Freddy asked if I had anything on me that identified me as a member of the organization. I did have one membership card to a subset organization and agreed to burn it. I had every intention of having the membership card replaced the next day.

Freddy asked Paula McClung, Vic's wife, for a container we could use to burn my membership card. Paula promptly gave Freddy a lid from a large mouth jar and a bath towel to put between the lid and the sofa. Freddy was convinced we would break the power of darkness in my home. I had zero confidence in what we were getting ready to do. I removed the card from my wallet and dropped it into the jar lid. And as soon as the card fell into the lid, my inward man, the hidden man of my heart, was transported twenty miles to the West into my house in Essex, Missouri.

I was standing in the archway between the hallway and the kitchen. I was facing a very ugly, gangly looking, hairy creature. He was sitting on the kitchen cabinets, between the cook stove and the kitchen sink. He was laughing out loud with some high-pitched, irritating voice. I did not say anything to the demon, but as soon as I realized what was happening in the spirit realm, I was immediately transported back to Vic's house.

Without hesitation, and without explanation, I quickly requested that we burn the card. I do not remember what we said, renounced, denounced or did as we burned the card, but it worked. We returned that evening to a very peaceful house. It was very pleasant to not have the unsettled atmosphere. We never had another demon manifestation in the house. We continued to live in that house until 1986 until we moved to Sikeston. I cannot explain it. I have just reported it. It is true as I have stated.

*Part 2*

# Post-Salvation Dreams and Visions

# 1

# 1979 February:
# God's Command
# Get on Radio - Get on TV

I was sitting at my kitchen table, the same one I use today, reading my Bible. I was looking out the south window across the backyard to Taylor Brother's farm shop. The Holy Ghost interrupted my reading by speaking into my heart. His voice was so clear it seemed audible to my natural ear; as though He was standing in the room with me. It sounded like a command.

*"Get on radio-Get on TV."*

The voice was so real. If I had turned and a person was standing there who had given the message, I would not have been surprised. The message was delivered supernaturally from God's Spirit to my spirit. It was so startling that I immediately shoved my chair back from the table as if to greet the person speaking. It was a *wow* moment that left me pondering what had I just heard from God.

Not to be outdone by a supernatural message from heaven, the devil stole my excitement with the supernatural voice of doubt, saying, *"You don't have the money to do this."* I had no idea the amount of money necessary to get on the radio, but the statement was true. I had no money. I sat down, almost in despair. When that much light of hope is snuffed out so quickly by darkness, it is quite painful.

As I pondered the reality of things, I sat down and pulled the chair back to its original position. I tried to resume reading, but the Word from God had branded me. My imagination of even the slightest of possibilities was burning in me like a raging forest fire.

The words of darkness were persistent, but I was so branded with hope I could not let go of God's words.

Sometimes after God delivers His message, He leaves me chewing on it to see if I will swallow. The more I chewed, the better it tasted, so I did swallow it and digested it.

Abraham had a similar experience. God promised him the impossible, but He expected Abraham to believe him and take action. After he finished his conversation with Abraham, He left him alone to chew on the Word He gave. Abraham wasted no time. He immediately began to obey God by moving forward with his part of the covenant. As he continued to chew on what God had said, he became fully persuaded that what God said, God would perform.

### Genesis 17:15-22 (KJV)

15 And God said unto Abraham, As for Sarai thy wife, thou shalt not call her name Sarai, but Sarah shall her name be. 16 And I will bless her and give thee a son also of her: yea, I will bless her, and she shall be a mother of nations; kings of people shall be of her. 17 Then Abraham fell upon his face, and laughed, and said in his heart, Shall a child be born unto him that is an hundred years old? and shall Sarah, that is ninety years old, bear? 18 And Abraham said unto God, O that Ishmael might live before thee! 19 And God said, Sarah thy wife shall bear thee a son indeed; and thou shalt call his name Isaac: and I will establish my covenant with him for an everlasting covenant, and with his seed after him. 20 And as for Ishmael, I have heard thee: Behold, I have blessed him, and will make him fruitful, and will multiply him exceedingly; twelve princes shall he beget,

and I will make him a great nation. <sup>21</sup> But my covenant will I establish with Isaac, which Sarah shall bear unto thee at this set time in the next year. <sup>22</sup> And he left off talking with him, and God went up from Abraham.

Within a couple of days, I went to a friend and mentor of mine, James Ross. I shared with him what I had heard about radio and TV. I knew James would pray about it and give me his counsel. We spent some time together talking about all God had said to me. We asked God for confirmation I had heard Him and guidance in moving forward.

I set a time of one week to seek God before I would return. I was excited all week, hoping James would call and say yes, you heard God. He did not call. I returned to his home at the appointed time. I was anxious and blurted out, *"What did you hear?"*

He answered, *"You are to be on radio and TV."* That was all I needed to launch out by faith into a ministry of which I was completely ignorant.

I did not know the necessary equipment, cost, procedure, etc. The first thing I did was contact our closest radio station to check for time and cost. I signed a binding annual contract with local radio station KDEX. I contracted to air a fifteen-minute program each weekday Monday through Friday.

I gradually learned more about the equipment as I used it. I quickly learned much more about the Bible. I am convinced that I learned more than the audience. Preparing the message, reading the Bible, meditation on what was revealed to my heart, and teaching was a great blessing to me. I was paying the radio station for my education. Oh, how I wish I had copies of those early teachings, but being frugal, we erased the masters as often as was possible to reuse them week after week for new programs.

We had no recording studio, so I would set up the recording equipment on a library table in the living room. After my family had gone to bed, I would record a full week of programs. I placed a box fan in the hallway toward the bedrooms to muffle the sound of the children. I had no way to edit so whatever came out of my mouth was recorded and aired. Sometimes I would fall asleep while recording and then come to myself while I was still speaking. The raw copy aired. Those were the days!

I was farming 1,000 acres, pastoring the congregation of Victory Temple Church in Dexter, Missouri and recording and airing five 15-minute radio programs per week. I had more energy than a stall-fed calf released into the pasture.

I have been teaching on radio and or TV since March 1979, and I have loved every minute of it. God has always shown Himself strong on my behalf with full provision.

> 2 Chronicles 16:9a (KJV)
> ⁹ For the eyes of the LORD run to and fro throughout the whole earth, to shew himself strong in the behalf of them whose heart is perfect toward him.

I did not ask for financial support, but all my expenses were covered. I was determined to not give the kingdom of God a bad name for being a beggar. I was so excited about God's abundant provision. I would pay a month in advance when I had the extra money. God has always honored my faithfulness by meeting all my need by His riches in glory by Christ Jesus.

On November 1, 2004, my wife and I purchased KLUH 90.3 FM, a 25,000 watt FM radio station in Poplar Bluff Missouri. It was a Southern Gospel music station when we purchased it. We changed the music format to Contemporary Christian music five months after the purchase date.

We bought it for the preaching of the gospel, and I am preaching on it every day of the year.

In only three years, we cleared the debt against the station. Then we began upgrading equipment to upgrade the audio quality. God has supernaturally provided all our needs as we have continued to practice the principle of sowing and reaping.

> 2 Corinthians 9:6-10 (KJV)
> 6 But this I say, He which soweth sparingly shall reap also sparingly; and he which soweth bountifully shall reap also bountifully. 7 Every man according as he purposeth in his heart, so let him give; not grudgingly, or of necessity: for God loveth a cheerful giver. 8 And God is able to make all grace abound toward you; that ye, always having all sufficiency in all things, may abound to every good work: 9 (As it is written, He hath dispersed abroad; he hath given to the poor: his righteousness remaineth forever. 10 Now he that ministereth seed to the sower both minister bread for your food, and multiply your seed sown, and increase the fruits of your righteousness;)

We were not only taught to sow the Word of God but also to give financially into good works of God. We have obeyed by sowing into other ministries, and again, God has honored His promises to us.

> Luke 6:38 (KJV)
> 38 Give, and it shall be given unto you; good measure, pressed down, and shaken together, and running over, shall men give into your bosom. For with the same measure

that ye mete withal, it shall be measured to you again.

Philippians 4:19 (KJV)
¹⁹ But my God shall supply all your need according to his riches in glory by Christ Jesus.

I did not get on TV until September 1983. In August 1983, I was driving west on Greer Street in Sikeston Missouri and was prompted to stop the car. I did, and thankfully no one rear-ended my vehicle. As I was trying to discern the reason for the prompting to stop abruptly in the middle of the street, I noticed a sign of Cable 6 Television Station to my right. I pulled over in a convenient parking place to investigate the TV station.

I was introduced to the owner *Nick the Greek.* Nick Zaharopolos gave me a list of the basic supplies of equipment and cost needed to air programs with him. I had no extra money for this project and had to do this by faith, just as I did the radio programming.

We were pioneering a church in Sikeston, Missouri with a small group of believers. Our first service was July 10th, twelve years to the Sunday of when I drowned in Milford Lake, Kansas. We were renting meeting rooms in the local Drury Inn Motel, sometimes in the bar room, sometimes in a banquet room, but it was all good.

The Sunday after meeting with Nick, I shared with the Church the instruction I had received in February 1979 to get on the radio and get on TV, and now we had before us an opportunity to take the next step in this life of faith.

The very next Sunday, Fred Moxley gave me a check for $5,000.00, and I felt like he had given me the key to the Fort Knox gold vault. Supernatural faith empowered me to obey what I heard in that supernatural message delivered to me in February 1979. I love it!

We purchased the equipment and within a couple of weeks were airing thirty-minute programs five days per week. Nick gave me some basic introductions of how to turn the equipment on and off, and away I went. I was so full of hope and faith that I was not sure I touched the ground when I walked!

My brother Joe Craig allowed me to use his photography studio at night to record my programs. I would record five programs for the next week, all alone in one filming session. At that time, I was farming 1,000 acres, recording five radio programs per week, recording five TV programs per week and pastoring Powerhouse of God Church.

I am rarely satisfied with my progress, so in November 1984, I contracted with TCT Television Network, Marion, Illinois and aired with them for twenty- six years. In the beginning, it was covering a local audience within a 45-mile radius of the station. Then, it progressed to a national market and then to an international audience of one billion five hundred million. President of TCT, Garth Coonce has always been very good to me.

One supernatural Word spoken by the Holy Spirit to my spirit has been enough to propel me to do radio and TV for thirty-eight years. Every day it is a supernatural walk of faith to continue these ministries, and God is always faithful to do His part. God and I both needed a partner, and I have gotten the better portion of this partnership. As long as I faithfully do my part, our partnership will produce much fruit that will remain.

John 15:1-8 (KJV)
I am the true vine, and my Father is the husbandman. 2 Every branch in me that beareth not fruit he taketh away: and every branch that beareth fruit, he purgeth it, that it may bring forth more fruit. 3 Now ye are

clean through the word which I have spoken unto you. *4 Abide in me, and I in you. As the branch cannot bear fruit of itself, except it abide in the vine; no more can ye, except ye abide in me. 5I am the vine, ye are the branches: He that abideth in me, and I in him, the same bringeth forth much fruit: for without me ye can do nothing.* 6If a man abide not in me, he is cast forth as a branch, and is withered; and men gather them, and cast them into the fire, and they are burned. 7If ye abide in me, and my words abide in you, ye shall ask what ye will, and it shall be done unto you. *8 Herein is my Father glorified, that ye bear much fruit; so shall ye be my disciples.*

# 2

# 1980:
# A Blaze of Glory

Since April of 1979, I had been asking the Lord about my place in ministry. It seemed that all my friends were getting personal prophecies, and I was disappointed that it was not happening to me. I did not recognize that the Holy Spirit was continuously revealing His will to me. It happened as I would enter into His presence with meditation, prayer, praise, or just simply reading the Scriptures. My life was a whirlwind of Holy Ghost activity, but it was Spirit to my spirit, not a personal prophecy from another Christian to me.

In January of 1980, Jesus appeared to me in an open vision in answer to my prayers. The Old Testament and the New Testament record God appearing to people with whom He needs to correspond. My experience was very scary to me. Even though I was sure of my salvation, His appearing caused a holy fear to fall upon me.

Judges 6:12 (KJV)

¹² And the angel of <u>the LORD appeared unto him,</u> and said unto him, The LORD is with thee, thou mighty man of valour.

Daniel 10:1-9 (KJV)

In the third year of Cyrus king of Persia a thing was revealed unto Daniel, whose name was called Belteshazzar; and the thing was true, but the time appointed was long: and he understood the thing and had understanding of the vision. ² In those days I Daniel was mourning three full weeks. ³ I ate no pleasant bread, neither came flesh nor wine in my mouth, neither did I anoint myself at all, till three whole weeks were fulfilled. ⁴ And in the four and twentieth day of the first month, as I was by the side of the great river, which is Hiddekel; ⁵ Then <u>I lifted up mine eyes, and looked</u>, and behold a certain man clothed in linen, whose loins were girded with fine gold of Uphaz: ⁶ His body also was like the beryl, and his face as the appearance of lightning, and his eyes as lamps of fire, and his arms and his feet like in colour to polished brass, and the voice of his words like the voice of a multitude. ⁷ And I Daniel alone saw the vision: for the men that were with me saw not the vision; but a great quaking fell upon them so that they fled to hide themselves. 8 Therefore I was left alone, and saw this great vision, and there remained no strength in me: for my comeliness was turned in me into corruption, and I retained no strength. 9 Yet heard I the voice of his words: and when I heard the voice of his words, then was I in a deep sleep on my face and my face toward the ground.

Acts 9:3-9 (KJV)

3 And as he journeyed, he came near Damascus: and suddenly there shined round about him a light from heaven: 4 And he fell to the earth and heard a voice saying unto him, Saul, Saul, why persecutest thou me? 5 And he said, <u>Who art thou, Lord</u>? And the Lord said, <u>I am Jesus whom thou persecutest:</u> it is hard for thee to kick against the pricks. 6 And he trembling and astonished said, Lord, what wilt thou have me to do? And the Lord said unto him, Arise, and go into the city, and it shall be told thee what thou must do. 7 And the men which journeyed with him stood speechless, hearing a voice, but seeing no man. 8 And Saul arose from the earth; and when his eyes were opened, he saw no man: but they led him by the hand and brought him into Damascus. 9 And he was three days without sight, and neither did eat nor drink.

Acts 10:1-7 (KJV)

There was a certain man in Caesarea called Cornelius, a centurion of the band called the Italian band, 2 A devout man, and one that feared God with all his house, which gave much alms to the people, and prayed to God alway. 3 He saw in a vision evidently about the ninth hour of the day an angel of God coming in to him, and saying unto him, Cornelius. 4 And when he looked on him, he was afraid, and said, What is it, Lord? And he said unto him, Thy prayers and thine alms are come up for a memorial before God. 5 And now send men to Joppa, and call for one Simon, whose surname is Peter: 6 He lodgeth with one Simon a tanner, whose house is by the sea side: he shall tell thee what thou oughtest to do. 7 And when the angel which spake unto Cornelius was departed, he called two of his household servants, and a devout soldier of them that waited on him continually;

My wife Harriet and I were invited to a prayer meeting in Dexter, Missouri. A few couples were gathering in a home to pray for a friend who was reportedly having some heart problems. I thought that was a strange request because the testimony of the year before was that God had given him a new heart. Harriet and I were the first guests to arrive. We were a little early because we intended to attend the prayer meeting and go on a date. We were so poor and had pinched our pennies so much you could read a newspaper through them, so our date was to be at the local Burger Chef.

We had interrupted the hosts' evening meal and excused ourselves to the living room, continuing to pray quietly in other tongues. As we were praying, people began gathering into the home. While sitting on the hearth of the fireplace, I continued to pray quietly in other tongues and briefly greeted the incoming guests as they were taking their seats. I did not engage in any lengthy conversations as I was primed to pray for our friend Dub Crutcher.

As the other couples were settling in, greeting one another and chatting before the meeting began, Jesus appeared to me in an open vision. The open vision allowed me to see into the realm of the spirit at the same time, as I was very conscious of all my natural surroundings. I could see Jesus and see and hear everyone in the room at the same time. While praying and observing the activity in the room, my attention had been drawn to the ceiling as a person was descending into the room. He seemed to be wearing loose fitting pants and a long robe that extended below his knees. His clothing was light colored and bright, maybe a light shimmering glow on the cloth. I followed his feet to the floor, and as His feet touched the floor, I was in the process of prostrating myself before Him. It seemed natural to me as I was overcome by His presence.

It was a holy fear that came upon me and caused me to prostrate myself before Him. No one else could see Him, and it seemed that everyone was still greeting each other as they were beginning to settle in for the time of prayer. Harriet was sitting beside me and was overcome by the Lord's presence, though she could not see Him in the vision. Another person, one of our good friends, Harry Glenn Williamson, who was filled with the Holy Ghost and was very sensitive and perceptive of the Lord's presence, must have recognized that I was seeing someone and was overcome by the holy presence. He spoke out with authority asked everyone to be quiet. When that happened, everyone quieted down, but I could no longer see Jesus. No one in the room but me could see Jesus, though I could see Him and all the people simultaneously. The vision ended without me receiving the intended message. I was so overcome by His presence that I do not remember the rest of the evening.

# *3*

# 1980 February:

In January, a friend of mine David Crank senior invited me to travel with his family to minister in Gary, Indiana. I traveled with him in February. Daily, since April 1979, I was questioning God about my place in ministry. On my return trip home from Saint Louis, MO, the Holy Ghost spoke to my spirit with the answer to my prayers.

I was traveling south on highway I-55 north of Cape Girardeau, Missouri, and I had just passed the rest stop when the Holy Spirit spoke to my spirit, "Begin to teach in Sikeston on a regular basis." I quickly followed up on that instruction and held a meeting within a few weeks in Sikeston, Missouri. Southeast Missouri was still very sensitive to the Charismatic movement. People were hungry for the presence of the Holy Spirit through prophecy, the laying on of hands, personal revelation and teaching on faith and healing.

Because of that supernatural revelation, I have been teaching in Sikeston, Missouri on a regular basis for thirty-eight years. God has not given me different instructions.

# 4

# 1980:
# Late February/early March
# Hearing the Call

After a very successful first meeting in Sikeston, I was still asking God for more clarification of my place in ministry. Shortly after that, He revealed to me, His Spirit to my spirit, **"You are an apostle and will operate in all of the fivefold ministry gifts."** That message was abundantly clear. However, I was still hung up on receiving a personal prophecy from some trusted person and was missing the answer to my question. Later in March or early April, I attended a meeting at the Kiel Auditorium, St Louis, Missouri. Between sessions, a lady turned me around at one of the product tables and said, "David, the Lord showed me that you are an apostle and will operate in all of the five-fold ministry gifts." This time I had my desire of a personal prophecy and the answer to my question. However, the devil had already infected my mind, and I would not receive it as the answer to my place in ministry.

The devil quickly nullified that revelation. Because of fear of man, my ignorance, and probably false pride, I said: "Lord, that would sound haughty coming from me, and I could never reveal that to anyone." I did not for many years. Though I did not understand the calling and purpose of an apostle, I can look back over the ministry and easily identify fruit borne from the office of apostle, prophet, teacher, and pastor. When placed in the proper settings for an evangelist, especially when ministering among people who are not overly familiar with me, the power gifts are released, and people are saved, healed, delivered from demons and secured in Christ.

Psalm 118:17 (KJV)
I shall not die, but live, and declare the works of the Lord.

Later in 1985, Hal Steenson, an apostle of God and close friend from West Frankfort, Illinois, spoke boldly to me to declare my office gifts and functions, but I did not. In 1996, in Kirksville Missouri, Steve Youngblood, an apostle, and Kevin Leal, a prophet, were adamant that I needed to declare my gifts, but I would not. In 2016, in Poplar Bluff Missouri, Graham Renouf, a prophet from New Zealand, declared I was a spearhead. I knew beyond the shadow of a doubt the meaning of that prophecy. Since my earliest ministry, I have operated in all five-fold ministry gifts.

Within the last year have I been declaring my office gifts and functions and the glory of God is being released afresh. The supernatural life is not something we can purchase. It is the life of all Christians, and for me to operate in my gifts and calling is necessary. I love living in the supernatural Life of God!

# 5

# 1980 July:
# I Command You to Live and Not Die

It was a hot and dry summer. It was so dry that when we cultivated our soybeans, we would laugh at ourselves because all we were doing was stirring up dust. After the crops were laid-by, we began a project to remove a farm building, one of our equipment storage sheds. I had helped my dad construct the building in the early 1960's but the supporting posts were rotting, and we were concerned the building might collapse. We had worked on it for some days, removing metal and boards we intended to salvage, and I was beginning to receive a warning that the building would fall on us.

On numerous occasions, I climbed on top of the building to inspect it and walk around its perimeter to locate the danger zone, but I never noticed it. The day the building fell, I had the strongest impression that it would come down that day. I did not want to scare anyone and did not say anything to anyone but was constantly trying to locate anything that would indicate the building would collapse.

Earlier that day I had taken a tractor to a neighbor farmer to borrow his three-point hitch, hydraulic lift boom to safely remove the larger trusses. I prayed the whole round trip but still could not locate the problem. We finally removed all the metal covering on the top and sides and began to remove the purlins by simply knocking them loose from the trusses. When only a few purlins remained, I asked Dean King to use one of the lighter and longer 2 X 4's to knock off more purlins. He was working from the underside standing on the ground.

Dean was busy removing purlins when he stopped and was about to say watch out. For a brief moment, the silence was deafening, and sure death was in the air. I assume that Dean had seen the building shift and begin to fall. He yelled the warning! I had been bent over using a wrecking bar to separate lumber that had been nailed together. An angel pulled me out to safety. Four of us, my sister Beth, her boyfriend and Dean King were all about forty feet inside the building. All three were trapped as the building came crashing down. Dean was killed.

The angel had removed me as far outside the building as I had been inside. I watched the trusses hit Dean. One truss hit the top of his head, and another hit the base of his neck. He was crushed in a sit-up position, with his face between his legs and to the ground. Seconds before he was crushed, he looked to his left,

70

directly at me, exhaled and died. Because I saw him killed, I did not even think about Beth or her boyfriend.

While the trusses were still bouncing from the fall, I was immediately at Dean's side flipping off the trusses that were crushing him. When the trusses were removed, I positioned myself in front of him. I grabbed his shirt and began to shake him back and forth violently while screaming, "I command you to live and not die! Death, come off him!" I must have screamed that command several times while I was shaking him. Blood had come out of his nose, mouth and maybe ears and he was not responding to my commands. I continued to shake him very violently, and finally, he gasped for breath.

He was in and out of consciousness until an ambulance could arrive 30-45 minutes later. He spent a few days in the Missouri Delta Hospital in Sikeston, Missouri. He was taking pain medication and was in a body brace. I could see that he was not improving. I convinced his mother to send him to Tulsa to the Kenneth E. Hagin Camp Meeting so that he could receive prayer from others. Apparently, I had maxed out my faith for the moment. Dean was very familiar with the teaching of faith in God to be healed. That fall, he was to be a second-year student at Rhema Bible Training Center, Broken Arrow, Oklahoma. He rode a bus to Tulsa and received prayer two or three times before he acted in faith. He removed the body brace to be found totally whole. Dean is currently a pastor with his wife and daughter in Atlanta, Georgia.

# 6

# 1980 August:
# Almost Crushed

I was delivered from death by an angel of God as he pulled me out from under a falling truck. I had my farm pickup truck in the farm shop to replace some brakes. I had lifted the truck by a dangerous jack, a "Handy Man" jack. That particular jack is handy for several applications, but it comes packaged with warnings of how not to use it. Once a person successfully uses any equipment incorrectly, without loss of life or limb, a bad habit is put into motion.

I had jacked up the truck from the rear bumper, just enough to remove the tires and wheels. I had forgotten to chock the front wheels to prevent the truck from rolling off the jack. Then I decided to lift the truck up as high as possible. With the jack fully extended, I proceeded to crawl under the truck to place the blocks under the axles. I had pushed the blocks under the truck before I crawled under it. I was reaching for a block to put in place when someone touched me very lightly on the back, about the level of my kidneys. The touch was lighter than a feather. It must have been an angel of God rescuing me! Without any conscious movement, I was out from under the truck, about ten feet behind it. I was standing up watching the truck crashing to the ground.

The truck had rolled forward, because the wheels had not been chocked, and the jack kicked out backward from its base. The jack was still turning a somersault in the air as the truck was crashing down. Again, I had been supernaturally delivered from great harm and possible death. I am convinced angels delivered me from death. Examples of this supernatural activity are recorded in the Bible.

Acts 12:5-12 (KJV)

⁵ Peter, therefore, was kept in prison: but prayer was made without ceasing of the church unto God for him. ⁶ And when Herod would have brought him forth, the same night Peter was sleeping between two soldiers, bound with two chains: and the keepers before the door kept the prison. ⁷ And, behold, the angel of the Lord came upon him, and a light shined in the prison: and he smote Peter on the side, and raised him up, saying, Arise up quickly. And his chains fell off from his hands. ⁸ And the angel said unto him, Gird thyself, and bind on thy sandals. And so he did. And he saith unto him, Cast thy garment about thee, and follow me. ⁹ And he went out and followed him; and wist not that it was true which was done by the angel; but thought he saw a vision. ¹⁰ When they were past the first and the second ward, they came unto the iron gate that leadeth unto the city; which opened to them of his own accord: and they went out and passed on through one street; and forthwith the angel departed from him. ¹¹ And when Peter was come to himself, he said, Now I know of a surety, that the LORD hath sent his angel, and hath delivered me out of the hand of Herod, and from all the expectation of the people of the Jews. ¹² And when he had considered the thing, he came to the house of Mary the mother of John, whose surname was Mark; where many were gathered together praying.

# 7

# 1980:
# The Sound of the
# Abundance of Rain

In the summer of 1980, Southeast Missouri was plagued with a terrible drought. We had gone weeks without any rainfall. In the early spring, I had begun a confession of perfect rainfall to begin after the crops were planted. My confession was we would receive one inch of rain every week. That did *not* happen!

One Saturday afternoon my family attended an annual barbeque at the Masonic Hall in Essex, MO. As we were purchasing our tickets, a man running for a Stoddard County political office gave me his card and chuckled saying, "If it rains, I will drop out of the race."

By the Holy Ghost, I said to him in a normal voice, "You had better drop out of the race. It is getting ready to rain one inch of rain."

He mockingly laughed saying, "You must have overhead irrigation."

I turned back to him and said, "No, I have flood irrigation," and then yelled at him, "You better drop out of the race! It is getting ready to rain one inch of rain here!" I was so loud that everyone stopped talking. After I yelled at the man, I was so high in the Holy Ghost I felt like I might not be touching the floor.

I had confessed one inch of rain per week after the crops were planted. However, drought was the rule of the day; until *that* day. By the grace of God, it began to rain and rained one inch of rain within the hour. No weather report was indicating rain, nor was there any natural indication of rain, but God supernaturally caused it to rain that day. I compare it to the story of drought in the days of Elijah the prophet.

> 1 Kings 18:41-46 (KJV)
> 41 And Elijah said unto Ahab, Get thee up, eat and drink; for there is a sound of abundance of rain. 42 So Ahab went up to eat and to drink. And Elijah went up to the top of Carmel; and he cast himself down upon the earth, and put his face between his knees, 43 And said to his servant, Go up now, look toward the sea. And he went up, and looked, and said, There is nothing. And he said, Go again seven times. 44 And it came to pass at the seventh time, that he said, Behold, there ariseth a little cloud out of the sea, like a man's hand. And he said, Go up, say unto Ahab, Prepare thy chariot, and get thee down that the rain stop thee not. 45 And it came to pass in the mean while, that the heaven was black with clouds and wind, and there was a great rain. And Ahab rode, and went to Jezreel. 46 And the hand of the LORD was on Elijah; and he girded up his loins, and ran before Ahab to the entrance of Jezreel.

Our tongue puts in motion the course of nature that affects us. I had practiced my confession for months with no apparent results. However, at the very moment God needed a group of people to see a miracle, he used that confession through me to gain their attention. Some of the community heard me say it, and some heard about it, but it was well-rehearsed in Essex. The next morning the miracle was being hotly debated in Ruth's Coffee Shop, Essex, Missouri.

R. D. Baker, who owned the retail lumber yard in Essex, had been standing very close to me when I said it. He was in the coffee shop the next morning participating in the discussions. 'Moose' Glen was not at the barbecue and did not hear me say it would rain one inch of rain. R. D. Baker heard me say it and told everyone, "I don't know how Doc knew it was going to rain, but it came to pass exactly as he said it would."

I needed it to come to pass to strengthen my faith, the unbelievers needed to see God alive and well on planet earth doing something supernaturally, and the farmers needed the rain.

Never underestimate the supernatural ability of your words, especially if they agree with God's promises. God supernaturally created things with words. Creation is supernaturally held together with words, so use them wisely.

James 3:2-6King James Version (KJV)
2 For in many things we offend all. If any man offend not in word, the same is a perfect man, and able also to bridle the whole body. 3 Behold, we put bits in the horses' mouths, that they may obey us; and we turn about their whole body. 4 Behold also the ships, which though they be so great, and are driven of fierce winds, yet are they turned about with a very small helm, whithersoever the governor listeth. 5 Even so the tongue is a little member, and boasteth great things. Behold, how great a matter a little fire kindleth! 6 And the tongue is a fire, a world of iniquity: so is the tongue among our members, that it defileth the whole body, and setteth on fire the course of nature; and it is set on fire of hell.

# 8

# 1982:
# I was Between Earth
# and Heaven

Some of my supernatural life may seem impossible to believe by the natural man, but if he is willing to read the Bible, he can see these types of supernatural activities were common.

As a Christian, I use Bible examples to help explain my supernatural life. Please compare my supernatural life to the Bible characters' supernatural life. Supernatural activity happens on the dark side, but I avoid using those examples. I am of the light, so I use examples that are of the light.

2 Corinthians 12:2-6 (KJV)
2 I knew a man in Christ above fourteen years ago, (whether in the body, I cannot tell; or whether out of the body, I cannot tell: God knoweth;) such an one <u>caught up to the third heaven</u>. 3 And I knew such a man, (whether in the body, or out of the body, I cannot tell: God knoweth;) 4 How that <u>he was caught up into paradise</u>, and heard unspeakable words, which it is not lawful for a man to utter. 5 Of such an one will I glory: yet of myself I will not glory, but in mine infirmities. 6 <u>For though I would desire to glory</u>, I shall not be a fool; for I will say the truth: <u>but now I forbear, lest any man should</u>

<u>think of me above that which he seeth me
to be, or that he heareth of me</u>.

I did not choose to go above the earth to see a vision from God. It was the means that God chose to show me His will. It is very easy for me to relate to the visions of the Prophet Ezekiel. My experiences are quite similar to his experiences.

Ezekiel 8:3 (KJV)
[3] And he put forth the form of an hand, and took me by a lock of mine head; and <u>the spirit lifted me up between the earth and the heaven</u>, and <u>brought me in the visions of God</u> to Jerusalem, to the door of the inner gate that looketh toward the north; where was the seat of the image of jealousy, which provoketh to jealousy.

This vision was short and happened while I was walking on a levee in my rice field in Lilbourn, Missouri. Rice is grown in water to nurture the plant and to deter the competing vegetation. The water level in the rice patties is critical and must be properly maintained. One of the levees would not hold water so, I suspected that some muskrats had burrowed tunnels through the levee, and it was draining the water down to the next rice patty. A simple method to locate the tunnels was to walk on top of the levee until it collapsed from my weight down into the tunnel.

As I walked along with my shovel to repair the levee, I was caught up in the Spirit. I saw an object fall from heaven through what appeared to be a glass shaft. I watched the object descend rapidly and strike what I thought was my rice field, but in the vision, it was a pool of golden liquid. The liquid appeared to be as a lightweight oil, heavier than water so as not to make a splash, but light enough to be easily penetrated. From the point at which the object struck the earth, I began ascending rapidly up into the heavens through the same shaft from which the object had descended to earth.

Waves began to form because of disturbance to the surface tension. When I first began to ascend, I could see the complete circle of the wave. Before the first wave was complete, my vision was limited to the north and east. I could see due north through Minnesota and due east through Virginia. The first wave ended just outside the northeast border of the United States, outside Nova Scotia. The second wave ended between Iceland and Greenland. The third wave ended inside Europe. The fourth wave ended on the eastern border of Finland. By the end of the fourth wave, I had ascended so high up into the heavens, that the earth disappeared to my vision.

The vision must have been very short in time as I did not fall from the very narrow levee. I was very puzzled and needed to share with someone, so I packed up my equipment and drove north to Sikeston to visit with my friend, Vic McClung. I shared the complete vision with him, and he answered, "I have no interpretation or understanding of what you're talking about." I returned to the rice field to repair the levee but could not shake the vision.

I looked at a flat map of the earth and began to realize that the waves were evenly spaced every 30 degrees. I went to our local high school, Richland High School and asked permission from Mr. Jim Lawrence to borrow or see a globe of the earth. Upon examining the globe, I could see the earth as I had seen it in the vision. In recent years, I have reviewed this vision many times by viewing the earth on 'google earth.'

My location on earth in the rice field of Lilbourn, Missouri was between 89-90 degrees. The first wave ended at about 60 degrees. The second wave ended at about 30 degrees. The third wave ended about 0 degrees. The fourth wave ended at about 30 degrees east. I shared the vision with a couple more people, but no one seemed to grasp it, and neither did I.

A few years later I was visiting with a friend living in Tulsa, Oklahoma. Danny and his wife were working for the T. L. Osborn Ministry. Danny was working for T. L. Osborn, and his wife was leading worship for Daisy Osborn. While visiting with Danny in the museum, we heard a door open on the West end, and as we turned, we saw T. L. Osborn walking in our direction. It pleased me that Danny offered to make the introduction.

When T.L. Osborn's and my hands grasped in the introduction, we never exchanged names. I quickly shared the vision with T.L. Osborn. He immediately interpreted the vision as a revival and encouraged me by shouting, "Go for it." He walked away to carry on his business. As of today, I have ministered in England, Wales, Ireland, Denmark, Sweden, Ukraine and Romania which are all in the footprint of the vision. The vision was used to relay, in a supernatural way, the will of God for me. I continue to seek God for greater interpretation of the vision and the part I play in it.

# 9

# Mid 1980's:
# What Shall Befall My People

Angels are supernatural beings that are ministering spirits for us. They have regions of creation under their influence. They protect us, and they deliver us from danger and death. They walk with us in times of harsh trials. They bring us messages, and they know one another. Those who rebelled against God remain in opposition to God and His will. Those who obeyed God remain faithful to God and His will. Sometimes, the opposing angels war with each other, and that is what I saw in the heavens.

Daniel 10:10-21 (KJV)
10 And, behold, <u>a hand touched me</u>, which set me upon my knees and upon the palms of my hands. 11 And he said unto me, O Daniel, a man greatly beloved, understand the words that I speak unto thee, and stand upright: for unto thee am I now sent. And when he had spoken this word unto me, I stood trembling. 12 Then said he unto me, Fear not, Daniel: for from the first day that thou didst set thine heart to understand, and to chasten thyself before thy God, thy words were heard, and I am come for thy words. 13 But the prince of the kingdom of Persia withstood me one and twenty days: but, lo, Michael, one of the chief princes, came to help me; and I remained there with the kings of Persia. 14 Now I am come to make thee understand what shall befall thy people in the latter days: for yet the vision is for many days. 15 And when he had spoken such words unto me, I set my face toward the ground, and I became dumb. 16 And, behold, one like the similitude of the sons of men touched my lips: then I opened my mouth, and spake, and said unto him that stood before me, O my lord, by the vision my sorrows are turned upon me, and I have retained no strength. 17 For how can the servant of this my lord talk with this my lord? for as for me, straightway there remained no strength in me, neither is there breath left

in me. <sup>18</sup> Then there came again and touched me <u>one like the appearance of a man</u>, and he strengthened me, <sup>19</sup> And said, O man greatly beloved, fear not: peace be unto thee, be strong, yea, be strong. And when he had spoken unto me, I was strengthened, and said, Let my lord speak; for thou hast strengthened me. <sup>20</sup> <u>Then said he, Knowest thou wherefore I come unto thee? and now will I return to fight with the prince of Persia: and when I am gone forth, lo, the prince of Grecia shall come</u>. <sup>21</sup> But I will shew thee that which is noted in the scripture of truth: and <u>there is none that holdeth with me in these things, but Michael your prince</u>.

I had several dreams of angelic warfare. In my first dream, I was working in my farm shop late at night repairing my combine to be ready for harvest. I could hear noise in the heavens, and I went out to see what was causing the noise. White and blue lights were moving across the havens so quickly that I could not turn my head fast enough to keep up with them. The lights formed formations of v's or triangles, like the formations of airplanes in our Air Force. They squared off into what I would describe as a dogfight. Then something in the heavens exploded with such volume that it shook me from my sleep, and my head was hurting as if a high-powered rifle had been fired near my ear. I cannot be sure of the interpretation, but many times it seemed to parallel struggles I was experiencing.

The weapons of our warfare are not carnal but mighty through God to the pulling down of strongholds. One of our great weapons is prayer, and one of the great methods of prayer is speaking in other tongues. In those years, I spoke much every day in tongues and had much resistance by darkness. However, I experienced great victory as I heard and obeyed God.

Daniel's prayers were being answered by God, but the powers of darkness were trying to prevent the answers from reaching Daniel's consciousness. Angels of darkness wanted Daniel's faith in God to fail. Angels of light wanted Daniel's faith in God to increase. Angels Michael and Gabriel fought against Daniel's adversaries.

Angels of God have been faithful in their assignment to me.

# *10*

# Mid to late 1980s: MMA in the Heavens

Christians are in a spiritual warfare! Does that scare you? Do you feel qualified to enter the ring? You are qualified in Christ to war a good warfare and win. You are a warrior for God in the battlefield of life on earth. Your general in heaven will relay messages to you in dreams. You need to know what your enemy is planning and the strategies to stop him. Angels will help bring you the messages and strategies from God.

Ephesians 6:10-20 (KJV)
10 Finally, my brethren, be strong in the Lord, and in the power of his might. 11 Put on the whole armour of God, that ye may be able to stand against the wiles of the devil. 12 For we wrestle not against flesh and blood, but against principalities, against powers, against the rulers of the darkness of

this world, against spiritual wickedness in high places. [13] Wherefore take unto you the whole armour of God, that ye may be able to withstand in the evil day, and having done all, to stand. [14] Stand therefore, having your loins girt about with truth, and having on the breastplate of righteousness; [15] And your feet shod with the preparation of the gospel of peace; [16] Above all, taking the shield of faith, wherewith ye shall be able to quench all the fiery darts of the wicked. [17] And take the helmet of salvation, and the sword of the Spirit, which is the word of God: [18] Praying always with all prayer and supplication in the Spirit, and watching thereunto with all perseverance and supplication for all saints; [19] And for me, that utterance may be given unto me, that I may open my mouth boldly, to make known the mystery of the gospel, [20] For which I am an ambassador in bonds: that therein I may speak boldly, as I ought to speak.

Through repetitive dreams, I received warnings of the plans of darkness against the United States of America. These particular dreams were given to me three times, and each time the dream was the same. The blue lights of heaven, as seen in earlier dreams, would come together to form the outline of a large jet airliner. While in the air, the jet airliner would explode, and the same lights would re-form into a square border with the words *Warning United States* inside the border. Because the dream came three times, I knew that tragedy was imminent for the airlines and passengers.

I shared the dreams on radio and television, but no one seemed to take notice. Within that year, jet airliners crashed because of explosions in the fuselage between the front of the wing and the cockpit. Some reasoned stress cracks were the problems for fuselage failure.

Later in the mid 90's a TWA airliner exploded not far off the USA's Northeast coast. Then on September 11, 2011, enemies of the United States of America commandeered four jet airliners to cause mass destruction.

I often wish that I had relationship with a greater network of those who share and interpret dreams, then follow life's events to determine their accuracy. Supernatural dreams and visions are for the entire body of Christ; whether someone is a prophet or not.

Share and compare your dreams and visions to determine their accuracy.

# 11

# Mid to late 1980s: Beyond the Levees

I saw a time when the three major river basins of the central USA were in flood stage at the same time. The Bible uses water in illustrations to describe activities of the Holy Ghost. I believe that in this particular dream, God was revealing His desire for a major demonstration of the power of God to come upon the earth.

Psalm 46:1-5 (KJV)
God is our refuge and strength, a very present help in trouble. 2 Therefore will not we fear, though the earth be removed, and

though the mountains be carried into the midst of the sea; ³ Though the waters thereof roar and be troubled, though the mountains shake with the swelling thereof. Selah. ⁴ *There is a river, the streams whereof shall make glad the city of God, the holy place of the tabernacles of the most High.* ⁵ God is in the midst of her; she shall not be moved: God shall help her, and that right early.

Isaiah 44:1-5 (KJV)

Yet now hear, O Jacob, my servant; and Israel, whom I have chosen: ² Thus saith the LORD that made thee, and formed thee from the womb, which will help thee; Fear not, O Jacob, my servant; and thou, Jesurun, whom I have chosen. ³ *For I will pour water upon him that is thirsty, and floods upon the dry ground: I will pour my spirit upon thy seed, and my blessing upon thine offspring:* ⁴ And they shall spring up as among the grass, as willows by the water courses. ⁵ One shall say, I am the LORD's; and another shall call himself by the name of Jacob; and another shall subscribe with his hand unto the LORD, and surname himself by the name of Israel.

Before and after this set of dreams I have had such dreams but nothing to this magnitude. In a dream, I saw a flood on the three large rivers in the central part of the United States (Missouri, Mississippi, & Ohio rivers) as they were all flooding at the same time. All the rivers were boiling and churning as their flood waters came through our region. The waters broke beyond the Mississippi River's levees and spread out over a vast region. As the rains lessened and the waters began to calm, the rich soils that were churning in the flood that had come from the northwest, north, and northeast, began to settle on our soil. This left behind great riches of topsoil that had come from other parts of the country.

Later, I began to reflect upon the contributing factors that cause a flood. Each stream of water has a head and a mouth. The head always receives a water supply from another stream or from over saturated ground that is shedding excess water. No river supplies its own water. It always receives its supply from another source and must give up its supply to an even greater source. All these rivers have personal identities in their local regions, identities they will always maintain locally, but as they give up their supply at their mouth to the next river, they are fulfilling their purpose though losing their identity.

Now their supply is joined with the supply of others, who lost their personal identities, until the final one supplied has such volume its energy can be harnessed to generate electric power to facilitate a better life with light, heat, air conditioning, and it can be used to irrigate crops that feed hungry people or provide places for recreation and pleasure. No supply is ever lost as it joins itself to another supplier to assist in meeting an even greater need.

> Ephesians 4:11-16 (KJV)
> 11 And he gave some, apostles; and some, prophets; and some, evangelists; and some, pastors and teachers; 12 For the perfecting of the saints, for the work of the ministry, for the edifying of the body of Christ: 13 Till we all come in the unity of the faith, and of the knowledge of the Son of God, unto a perfect man, unto the measure of the stature of the fulness of Christ: 14 That we henceforth be no more children, tossed to and fro, and carried about with every

wind of doctrine, by the sleight of men, and cunning craftiness, whereby they lie in wait to deceive; 15 But speaking the truth in love, may grow up into him in all things, which is the head, even Christ: 16 From whom the whole body fitly joined together and compacted by that which <u>every joint supplieth</u>, according to the effectual working in the measure of every part, <u>maketh increase of the body</u> unto the edifying of itself in love.

I believe it is the will of God that individual receives the glory of God to excess and overflowing. He is to share it with another individual who will repeat the process. Through this process, the body of Christ will increase in size and power until it is desired to supply the needs of the world. In this dream, all three of these rivers ultimately became one river--the Mississippi River. In the kingdom of God, it is the River of Life.

Psalm 46:4 KJV
There is a river, the streams whereof shall make glad the city of God, the holy place of the tabernacles of the most High.

The body of Christ begins as a mustard seed sown into good ground and produces the largest herb in the garden where even the fowl of the air finds food and rest. Each Christian is very significant to all of life. We do have the "butterfly effect" on society. If each of us allows our seed to grow to maturity, we can bless our lost and dying world.

Mark 4:30-32 (KJV)
30 And he said, Whereunto shall we liken the kingdom of God? or with what

comparison shall we compare it? [31] It is like a grain of mustard seed, which, when it is sown in the earth, is less than all the seeds that be in the earth: [32] But when it is sown, it groweth up, and becometh greater than all herbs, and shooteth out great branches; so that the fowls of the air may lodge under the shadow of it.

# *12*

# 1984 February:
# The Coat of the King

Lester Sumrall laid hands on me in the hallway of Faith Church, St Louis Missouri. Ron Tucker was the pastor. When hands were laid on me, a glorious anointing came upon me and formed like a two-inch thick Eisenhower Jacket.

Numbers 27:18-23 (KJV)
[18] And the LORD said unto Moses, Take thee Joshua the son of Nun, a man in whom is the spirit, and <u>lay thine hand upon him</u>; [19] And set him before Eleazar the priest, and before all the congregation; and give him a charge in their sight. [20] And thou shalt <u>put some of thine honour upon him,</u> that all the congregation of the children of Israel may be obedient. [21] And he shall stand before Eleazar the priest, who shall ask counsel for him after the judgment of Urim before

the LORD: at his word shall they go out, and at his word they shall come in, both he, and all the children of Israel with him, even all the congregation. 22 And Moses did as the LORD commanded him: and he took Joshua, and set him before Eleazar the priest, and before all the congregation: 23 And he laid his hands upon him, and gave him a charge, as the Lord commanded by the hand of Moses.

This was another good year for me to receive increased anointing by the laying on of hands of the presbytery. In January, Vic McClung had been reading some radical fasting material from author Franklin Hall and asked if I would join him in a fast. I agreed with him but did nothing to change my diet in preparation for a total fast of twenty-one days. Vic had prepared, but I had not. However, God was good to me. During the first few days, I thought my head would explode due to withdrawal from caffeine and sugar. I continued to do all my farm work for the twenty-one days without any weakness.

About halfway through the fast, I was impressed to have Lester Sumrall lay hands on me. I had been introduced to some real demonic activity and did not like to deal with it. As a pastor, I need to deal with all problems. By encouragement of the Holy Ghost, I expected that when Lester Sumrall laid hands on me something good would happen, but I had the surprise of my life. I had come to the meeting for the specific reason for the laying on of hands. I came for the specific purpose that I would no longer be afraid to minister to truly demonized people.

It is possible to receive increased Holy Ghost activity from another person: Moses to Joshua; Elijah to Elisha; David to Solomon; Jesus to His apostles; Paul to Timothy. Lester Sumrall's testimonies indicated that he had no fear of devils and had cast out many. I needed what he had and expected to receive from him.

Lester Sumrall's aid and or pilot set up the meeting for me. He was to pray for me at the end of ministry of that evening. I expected him to pray for me before the whole congregation. That did not happen. Lester Sumrall closed his session and walked out of the sanctuary. The pilot gathered Lester Sumrall's personal items, and they disappeared. I was deflated. I was sure the Holy Ghost had instructed me to locate him to have him lay hands on me.

Within a few minutes, the pilot returned to retrieve me for a private audience with Lester Sumrall. It was not a fancy introduction and exchange of pleasantries. It was simply business. We met in the hallway outside Pastor Tucker's office. The pilot introduced me by name and stated briefly my purpose for the meeting. Lester Sumrall was about my height. He looked directly into my eyes. He poked around on the billfold I carried in my shirt pocket under my sweater. Maybe he was checking to see if I was carrying cigarettes. He finished his examination then briefly stared at me. Then he extended his hand forcefully toward me, shouting receive! I did.

I have no memory of actually being touched by him, but I collapsed to the floor. It was not a charismatic courtesy fall with a catcher. It was a slam to the carpet covered concrete floor. My eyes and ears remained functional, but I could not move a single muscle, nor could I speak words. I remained alone on the floor for several minutes. People were leaving the building to fellowship with Lester Sumrall.

My upper body felt cloaked from my neck to my waste in an Eisenhower jacket that was two inches thick. The overwhelming presence of the Holy Ghost anointing lasted for hours. I did not know if I was on earth or suspended somewhere between heaven and earth. After that night, to this day in 2018, I can refresh that anointing by meditating upon that event. When I invite that anointing, God uses me more powerfully in words of knowledge, words of wisdom, prophecies, and healings.

# 13

# 1984:
# The House Exploded
# and Burned

Terry is a childhood friend of mine and a Vietnam veteran. He spent two years as a point man in the bush and came home scarred from war. After his wedding to the love of his life and reception ceremony, he had returned home. They were changing into some more comfortable clothing to go on a honeymoon and did not smell the natural gas that had filled his house in his absence.

At one point he lit a cigarette, and the house exploded. He gathered his wife's burning body and removed her from the house. Both had third-degree burns on much of their flesh. He and his wife were immediately taken to a hospital in Memphis, TN. They were to be stabilized and transferred on to the Burn Center at Fort Sam Houston, San Antonio Texas.

We received a phone call from other friends living in Clover Bend Arkansas, asking for prayer. My parents came to my house with the story, and we immediately began to pray. I knew by the Holy Ghost that Terry would live and not die and declared that verse, this sickness is not unto death. I had received a supernatural gift of faith to declare his recovery.

John 11:4 King James Version (KJV)
⁴ When Jesus heard that, he said, This sickness is not unto death, but for the glory of God, that the Son of God might be glorified thereby.

Psalm 118:17 (KJV)
    ¹⁷I shall not die, but live, and declare the works of the LORD.


Terry survived, but his wife died. Terry continues to live in the community in which he was born and raised. After much delay, he has remarried.


# *14*

# 1984 November:
# Death Come Off Him

When traveling on tour to Israel with Lester Sumrall, I was delivered from death. Ed Dufresne laid hands on me in a hotel ballroom, Jerusalem Israel and the spirit of death came off me. Disobedience will open a person to an attack of demons and even death that God will not stop unless they repent.

I had been given instructions in 1980 to enter into fulltime ministry. I was to dissolve my partnership with my dad and leave the farming business. I was the one who initiated the partnership, and now I had to dissolve it. We were increasing in our blessings and assets, so I did not know how to dissolve the partnership. I asked my mother to intervene for me, but she would not.

I tried to go to Rhema Bible Training Center to break the contract. I did not. During the tour of the school, Mrs. Lynette Hagin invited me into the lounge for a cup of coffee and introduced me to one of the teachers. A teacher confronted me about my purpose for becoming a student, and I did not have a ready answer. I went home to inform my wife that we would not be going to Rhema Bible

Training Center. Finally, I just dropped the idea of dissolving the partnership. The door of death had been opened in my life, and the angel of death did not leave until he was driven out.

I first noticed the spirit of death as very lightweight. It was as light as a feather, maybe even as a fly, as it landed on my left shoulder. I looked toward my shoulder and brushed off the unseen weight, but it did not leave. I became aware that death had taken hold of me, but I did not know how it had happened. Over the next year, the weight increased many-fold. I began to pray, repent, beg, anything I could do to get God's attention. I desperately desired to be free from this attack, but death was steadily gaining a stronger hold on my life. Finally, I purchased some life insurance to provide for my family after my anticipated demise.

One day Harriet came into where I was praying and dropped her face into my lap sobbing tears saying, "You are dying aren't you?" I answered in the affirmative. She questioned if had prayed. I informed her that I had prayed, repented of every sin I could dredge up and was now repenting of things I was not sure I had done. I was covering all my bases. It was almost like the time I was drowning in Milford Lake, calling for the rescuers, but none were coming to my aid. But God had a plan!

While attending a building dedication of my friend David Crank Sr. in St Louis Missouri, God began to reveal the plan. David had invited Lester Sumrall as the speaker for the special service. As he was encouraging people to go to Israel with him, the Holy Ghost spoke up inside of me and said, "I will speak to you in Jerusalem."

I immediately responded. "Lord, I hear your voice. Talk to me now." The Lord did not speak of the divine appointment again. I immediately set some parameters to hear God. I will hear Your voice by Holy Spirit to my spirit, by reading the Scriptures, or by a trusted person of God that does not know me personally. Death continued daily to work toward my destruction. Nothing changed until November in Jerusalem, Israel.

I believe it was the sixth night in Israel, the third night in Jerusalem that Ed Dufresne spoke to those of us in the banquet hall. He said that Dr. Sumrall had requested that he share a testimony in his life. He shared how he had been disobedient to God and death had taken hold of him. Ed ended the testimony declaring, "Two men in here are disobedient to God, and if you do not repent you will be dead within six months." I ran to the front to receive prayer.

When he laid his hands on me and rebuked death, the heavy weight lifted, and I was as light as I was the moment I gave my life to Christ. It was not until then I realized how death had taken hold of me. By not obeying God's direction to get out of the farming business, the devil had the legal right to attack me. Thank God I was allowed to live until someone could help me. God had worked with my parameters of receiving a Word by the Holy Ghost. Ed Dufresne was a trusted minister that had no personal knowledge of my life.

It was not until I had returned to my Church, Powerhouse of God, that I became aware I had also received another Holy Ghost impartation. The impartation happened as Ed Dufresne laid hands on me to free me from death. The healing anointed had increased. After that impartation, I began to walk like Ed Dufresne while I was ministering. I did not understand what had happened and why I was now walking like Ed Dufresne. I almost killed that impartation thinking I had picked up a familiar spirit that was imitating Ed Dufresne's walk through me. God was in the whole thing, and I am alive and doing well with an even greater anointing to heal the sick, cleanse the leper, raise the dead and cast out devils.

The present-day distortion of the meaning of God's love, denying God will correct the people he loves, is a very dangerous doctrine. God had not sentenced me to death! Satan is the murderer. Satan came in and had taken hold of my life through the door of my disobedience. If I had not repented of my rebellion, I would have died young and missed my purpose in life.

If we pay attention to the warning in this Psalm, we can free God to bless us to save our life!

95

Psalm 78:41 (KJV)

<sup>41</sup> Yea, they <u>turned back</u> and <u>tempted God</u>, and limited <u>the Holy One of Israel</u>.

Our disobedience prevents or hinders God's legal right to bless us. Do not be afraid to present yourself before God for inspection. By use of x-ray and MRI, the medical community will often inspect things hidden from their sight or understanding. We need to ask God to search our hearts to reveal things out of order.

God spoke to me supernaturally while Lester Sumrall was encouraging people to travel with him to Israel. Before I could receive further instruction, I had to go to Jerusalem. The supernatural life requires *hearing* from God and *obeying what we hear*.

Psalm 139:23-24King James Version (KJV)

<sup>23</sup> Search me, O God, and know my heart: try me, and know my thoughts: <sup>24</sup> And see if there be any wicked way in me, and lead me in the way everlasting. God revealed my disobedience, my sentence and my door of freedom, repentance. I heard! I obeyed! I have stayed!

# 15

# February 1987:
# Your Momma Will Die

I received the warning of my mother's death while attending a church service in West Frankfort, Illinois.

I had been working on a telethon for TCT and was exhausted at the end of the day. I needed to be renewed in the presence of God. I attended the church of a very good friend of mine, Apostle Hal Steenson. During the praise & worship service, an older gentleman in the row before me raised both of his hands as he praised the Lord. As I viewed the back of his raised hands, the Lord opened my heart to see my mother's death. He said, "Your mother will die, and you will not be able to stop it." I was stunned and remained silent!

> 2 Kings 20:1 (KJV)
> In those days was Hezekiah sick unto death. And the prophet Isaiah the son of Amoz came to him, and said unto him, Thus saith the LORD, <u>Set thine house in order; for thou shalt die, and not live</u>.

Later, I cried, and I prayed for six months arguing my case with God, but to no avail. God never spoke to me again concerning the matter, and mom's death came to pass as He had spoken.

After I was convinced that mom would die, and we would not be able to stop it, I told my dad in August of 1987. Dad was standing beside his pickup truck and collapsed as I shared the news. He was able to catch himself on the bed of the pickup truck before falling to the ground. He could not believe it was going to happen as the Lord had said. He thoroughly questioned me if I had truly heard God. I had heard clearly.

God did not give me a reason as to why mom would die. Momma died in February 1988, and I did her funeral. It was the hardest funeral for me, even harder than when my older sister had been murdered. I am glad God had prepared us for her death.

# 16

# Late 1980s: Praying from God's Position

God needs Christians to pray! Through our prayers, God can prevent tragedies, open men's hearts to receive Him, and answer other people's prayers. I choose to pray. I obey the call to pray. Sometimes, I am chosen to pray. Praying from God's position, standing between earth and heaven, is a supernatural manifestation of the Holy Spirit. I did not ask for this position nor did I do anything to deserve this opportunity. It was God's doing.

> Ezekiel 22:30 (KJV)
> 30 And I sought for a man among them, that should make up the hedge, and stand in the gap before me for the land, that I should not destroy it: but I found none.

> Romans 8:24-26 (KJV)
> 24 For we are saved by hope: but hope that is seen is not hope: for what a man seeth, why doth he yet hope for? 25 But if we

hope for that we see not, then do we with patience wait for it. 26 Likewise the Spirit also helpeth our infirmities: for we know not what we should pray for as we ought: but the Spirit itself maketh intercession for us with groanings which cannot be uttered.

Acts 11:5 (KJV)
5 I was in the city of Joppa praying: and in a trance I saw a vision, A certain vessel descend, as it had been a great sheet, let down from heaven by four corners; and it came even to me:

Ephesians 6:18-19 (KJV)
18 Praying always with all prayer and supplication in the Spirit, and watching thereunto with all perseverance and supplication for all saints; 19 And for me, that utterance may be given unto me, that I may open my mouth boldly, to make known the mystery of the gospel,

Jude 20-23 (KJV)
20 But ye, beloved, building up yourselves on your most holy faith, praying in the Holy Ghost, 21 Keep yourselves in the love of God, looking for the mercy of our Lord Jesus Christ unto eternal life. 22 And of some have compassion, making a difference: 23 And others save with fear, pulling them out of the fire; hating even the garment spotted by the flesh.

I was standing in the heavens, far above the eastern border of Finland. This position was the end of the fourth wave in the dream of 1982. I was crying over Russia, praying and interceding in other tongues. I did not know how I had ascended into the heavens above the eastern border of Finland. I had not been forewarned of this event and was not sure of my assignment in prayer.

I wept bitterly for a long time with no understanding. Within a few years, the government of Russia began to unravel. I am glad that God unites his people in prayer, through the Holy Ghost, to accomplish His will. Surely many others from around the world had also received and were actively engaged in this prayer assignment concerning Russia.

It was later that I gained more understanding of this prayer. I will share further in the next vision.

# *17*

# Later in the 1980s: Setting the Captives Free

I saw a political prisoner set free.

Anna Chercova was tormented by the KGB because of her life in Christ. She was probably one of many that were suffering as a witness for Jesus Christ under communist rule. Her plight was brought to me by a person in our prayer group. Our group prayed together every Monday-Friday, 8:30 AM-10:00 AM. Daily, as I sat behind my pulpit, my place of prayer, I reviewed the names of the persecuted. The request was before me, but I had no compelling desire to address it. I hate to admit it, but I ignored the request for some months.

One day, as I had pulled out the request, compassion broke over my soul, and I cried out for her freedom and deliverance.

Immediately I was taken far above the earth, as when I was above the eastern border of Finland. From my position in heaven/space, I saw a light come on in Russia. I believe the light was in the vicinity of Moscow. A beam of light came from that location in Russia up to and beyond my position in heaven. I rejoiced and told the prayer group to stop praying for Anna Chercova.

By a supernatural gift of faith, I rejoiced for her freedom. I was fully persuaded she had been released from prison! This whole prayer was the supernatural orchestration of God. I did not know the woman. I had no natural inclination to pray for the woman. For months I had no desire to pray for the woman. Then, at least it seemed to be then, I cried out for her deliverance, and God honored the prayer. In reflection, I might have been interceding for her when I was crying over Russia. None the less, her prayer for deliverance was granted. I am thankful I was selected to participate on God's prayer team. All glory to God!

No one understood my explanation of how I had come to that conclusion. Within a few weeks after seeing the vision, we discovered physical evidence that it was true. While visiting with my wife's family in North Little Rock, Arkansas, Harriet read an article covering Anna Chercova's release. Harriet laminated the newspaper article along with the prayer request. It has always served as a great reminder of my usefulness in prayer. When the devil cranks up his propaganda machine against my soul, I reflect on this supernatural life event.

# WOMEN IN SOVIET PRISON CAMPS NEED YOUR CONTINUED PRAYERS AND LETTERS

Arrested in August, 1973, Anna Vasilievna Chertkova, 58, may spend the rest of her life imprisoned for her belief in God. Anna was tried December 2, 1974, charged with slandering the Soviet state and social order and sentenced to treatment in a special psychiatric hospital.

A member of an unregistered Baptist church, Anna was arrested for evangelism and the distribution of religious books. She now spends her days undergoing the same inhumane treatment as her fellow inmates, most of whom are actual lunatics and/or murderers. She is subjected to forced injections, beatings and other tortures from the orderlies and KGB psychiatrists who are given free reign to beat, rape, and rob the inmates. Forced injections of sulfazine (a mixture of sulfur and peach oil that has only one purpose — to inflict severe pain) have resulted in permanent body tremors.

Early in 1986, after having spent 12 years in the Tashkent Special Psychiatric Hospital, Anna was taken in handcuffs to the Kazan Special Psychiatric Hospital, an equally horrible facility. Anna has apparently been able to maintain her mental faculties, but her body has been ravaged by extreme physical abuse. Because Anna's sentence is indefinite, without a miracle it is possible that she will never be released. The Soviets, under law, can keep her until she no longer shows any sign of "madness" (i.e., belief in God).

Anna Chertkova is one of many prisoners persecuted for their love of God. Below is an updated list of prisoners who need prayer and letters. Pressure from the West to see these people released has already produced results. Over the past year, several prisoners have been released through the power of prayer and the power of the pen.

According to reports from the Slavic Gospel Association, approximately 230 Christians remain in prison for their beliefs and, undoubtedly, there are many more. We cannot be satisfied with the victories already experienced; we

*Anna Vasilievna Chertkova*

must continue our efforts. Please write Mikhail Gorbachev, address him as "Your Excellency," and tell him of your concern for a particular prisoner, calling him or her by name. Also, write the Russian Ambassador to the United States. The addresses are below.

In writing letters to the prisoners and their families, offer words of encouragement and quote comforting Scriptures. Tell them of your prayers and the prayers of thousands of Christians around the free world. Use a plain white envelope, hand printing the address on the front and your own address on the back. Write in English, unless you know the Russian language well. Send your letters by registered mail, return receipt requested. Whether or not your letters are received by the prisoners, rest assured they will be read by Soviet authorities. Your letter and prayers can make the difference in the lives of people imprisoned for their faith.

*For more information on the Slavic Gospel Association, write P.O. Box 1122, Wheaton, IL 60189, (312) 690-8900.*

Address letters of protest to:
Secretary Mikhail Gorbachev
The Kremlin
Moscow, R.S.F.S.R.
SOVIET UNION

The Hon. Yuri Dubrinin
Embassy of the U.S.S.R.
1125 16th St., N.W.
Washington, D.C. 20036

## RUSSIAN WOMEN IMPRISONED FOR THEIR FAITH

CHERTKOVA, Anna
420082 Tatarskaya
Ass R, g. Kazan, ul
Yershova 49, uchr.
UE-148/st. 6-14 otd.

HERZEN, Susanna
722169 Kirghizskaya SSR,
Alamedinsky raion,
s. Stepnoye, uchr. OP-32/2-6-61
*(Arrested 4/22/85)*

TARASOVA, Zinaida
278540 Moldavskaya SSR.
Kotovsky raion,
pos. Ruseka, uchr.
OShch 29/7-4
SOVIET UNION
*(Arrested after discovery of printing press for Christian publishing service. Arrested 10/17/85.)*

VELIKANOVA, Tatyana
Kazakhskaya SSR,
465070 Mangyshlakskaya obl.,
pos. Beineu, do vostrebovaniya
SOVIET UNION
*(In exile; charged with anti-Soviet agitation and propaganda)*

ZHUKOVSKAYA, Evelina
429430 Chuvashskaya ASSR, g.
Kozlovka,
uchr. YuL 34/5-25 "Y"
SOVIET UNION
*(Baptist, due to be released 5/13/88)* ☐

by Kimberly Parker

# Soviets punishing Christians

WASHINGTON — While Mikhail Gorbachev is wooing hearts with his new openness, Vasili Shipilov is passing his 48th year in Soviet labor camps and psychiatric hospitals. His crime? Shipilov is a Christian.

The 65-year-old Russian Orthodox believer is one of 169 Christians who will spend this Christmas imprisoned in the Soviet Union for a variety of crimes against the state that can be boiled down to the practice of religion. Religious prisoners are released by the Soviets in a trickle that makes the most out of Gorbachev's glasnost public relations program — one or two before summit talks, another on the eve of human rights conferences.

Jewish refuseniks get the lion's share of attention in this country because their supporters here are highly motivated by fresh memories of the Holocaust and because the Soviet Jews want out of their country. But Christians in the Soviet Union, for the most part, don't want out. They just want to attend church in their homeland. And their fellow Christians in this country have not taken up their cause.

Anglican priest Richard Rodgers told our associate, Daryl Gibson, the cheerless story of Vasili Shipilov.

He was first arrested in 1939 as a 17-year-old seminarian and sentenced to 10 years in a labor camp. He was released in 1949 but was arrested again the same year for preaching Christianity and criticizing Joseph Stalin in Siberia. He was subsequently diagnosed variously as schizophrenic and epileptic and confined to psychiatric hospitals. He was once told he would remain a prisoner until he denounced his faith. He hasn't.

The Institute on Religion

Jack Anderson

and Democracy at Keston College in England, which keeps track of religious prisoners, reported that Shipilov is beaten when he crosses himself or observes a religious fast.

In 1979, Shipilov was discharged from a psychiatric hospital and, since he has no family, he was ordered to go to a home for invalids. The home had a long waiting list, so Shipilov couldn't leave the hospital. Keston College officials believe he is still being held prisoner in the hospital in Siberia, 48 years after he was snatched from the seminary.

Rodgers has taken up the cause of Vasili Shipilov. Rodgers is a former orthopedic surgeon who gave up medicine for the ministry when he learned of the plight of Soviet Christians.

In 1986, he shaved his head, fashioned a "cell" and sat in the cell in a church in Birmingham, England, eating only bread and water for 48 days during Lent. He wanted to simulate the conditions of Soviet Christian poet Irina Ratushinskaya, in prison for "subverting and weakening the Soviet regime." She was released by Gorbachev as a friendly gesture before the Iceland summit in 1986.

Four days before Gorbachev arrived in the United States for the White House summit, Baptist Anna Chertkova was released after 14 years in a psychiatric hospital. Several times during her term she was told, "Deny God and you will be home tomorrow."

The handful of U.S. Christian groups following this cause have more horror stories to tell — a teen-ager beaten at school for being a Christian; healthy prisoners injected with psychiatric drugs; a Baptist declared mentally unstable and socially dangerous for distributing religious leaflets; two Catholic fathers sentenced to 10 years each for organizing a Christmas party for parish children and preaching sermons against social ills; attempts by the KGB to recruit seminarians as informants; confiscation of churches, which are then turned into warehouses, concert halls or "museums of atheism." The list goes on.

According to the congressional Human Rights Caucus, there are at least 17 ways the Soviets grind their heels into religious believers. They range from prohibitions against teaching religion to minors to job discrimination against believers. Because religion and communism are natural enemies, it is easy for officials to come up with a formal charge that the believer threatens the foundations of the government.

In August, Sen. Richard Lugar, R-Ind., extracted a promise from Konstantin Kharchev, chairman of the Soviet Council for Religious Affairs, that all "prisoners of faith" would be released by November. Kharchev made the same promise to Jaime L. Cardinal Sin of Manila and added that 12 new Catholic churches would open in September. Neither promise was kept.

Lugar is sending another envoy to Kharchev. In the meantime, the speculation on Capitol Hill is that the Soviets will continue to release religious prisoners when it benefits their public image.

# 18

# 1988 July August:
# Apologize to Mr. X

Are you aware that un-forgiveness will separate you from God's blessings? Think about it! Matthew 5:43-48 has not always been my go-to scripture when progress is grinding to a halt. It is becoming more apparent that if these scriptures are disobeyed or ignored, it can be a game stopper for the ministry and personal life. I argued my case as to why it was not my responsibility to apologize to Mr. X. I am glad I lost my case. I learned a lot through the process. Being cheated, being offended, being tested to forgive continues to this day. Will it ever end while living on earth in this age? Probably not.

Our church, Powerhouse of God Church, had its first service on July 10, 1983. It was twelve years to the Sunday of when I had drowned in Milford Lake Kansas, just outside Fort Riley Kansas. After about a year as a newly formed congregation, we desired to purchase property to construct our own sanctuary. To our surprise, we discovered that the city of Sikeston, Missouri had covenants preventing churches from being constructed on newly developed residential properties.

Terry Collins, a local realtor, had offered to sell us some of their commercial property. Before our leaders could come to an agreement to purchase the property, it was purchased by another firm. As we continued searching for property, we continued to receive donations toward the purchase of land and construction of buildings. However, we continued to be resisted by property owners.

No one ever explained why it appeared that we were being shut out. Finally, a new area was being developed for light industrial industries, and we inquired about an opportunity. The land manager was very cordial, and I did not haggle over the price, so I thought we were finally in the game. When he asked our intention for the property, discussions stopped, and everything closed against us.

I would not accept defeat! I countered with an aggressive questioning and decided to go above the manager to the owners. I was sure that I had won, but to my dismay, we suffered further set-back. Even the offerings suffered, especially ones designated to purchase property. We understood the principle of sowing and reaping, so we agreed to sow into another ministry. We considered them to be good ground. We sowed all that we had received toward the purchase of property. Still, nothing changed. We were at a standstill and maybe sliding backward.

Please pay attention! Obedience in one area does not guarantee that God will overlook disobedience in another area. Becoming a soul winner will not guarantee that God will turn a blind eye to fornication. Our sowing did not overcome my offense and disobedience of not forgiving. Are these tough examples? I believe you get the point.

In one of our 8:30-10:00 AM, Monday through Friday prayer meetings, the Holy Ghost spoke very clearly, "Go and apologize to Mr. X." He was the land manager. I rehearsed God's command and my resentment. I believed we had been falsely accused and ill-treated. I argued my case. No! I refused to obey God. Obviously, God did not yield to my foolishness.

God was gracious and gave me another opportunity on the second day. I was just as crazy as the first day. No! God again did not answer my foolishness. God was very gracious and gave me another opportunity on the third day. I almost blew it again, but stopped myself short and said, "I will do it." Admittedly, it was not the kindest letter of apology, but God honored my obedience. The land manager had a change of heart, and the land was quickly sold to us.

Deuteronomy 28:1-14 (KJV)

And it shall come to pass, **if thou shalt hearken diligently unto the voice of the Lord thy God**, to <u>observe</u> and to <u>do all</u> his commandments which I command thee this day, that the Lord thy God will set thee on high above all nations of the earth: **2** And all these blessings shall come on thee, and overtake thee, **if thou shalt hearken unto the voice of the Lord thy God.**

**3 Blessed** shalt thou be in the city, and blessed shalt thou be in the field.

**4 Blessed** shall be the fruit of thy body, and the fruit of thy ground, and the fruit of thy cattle, the increase of thy kine, and the flocks of thy sheep.

**5 Blessed** shall be thy basket and thy store.

**6 Blessed** shalt thou be when thou comest in, and **blessed** shalt thou be when thou goest out.

**7** The Lord shall cause thine enemies that rise up against thee to be smitten before thy face: they shall come out against thee one way, and flee before thee seven ways. **8** The Lord shall command the blessing upon thee in thy storehouses, and in all that thou settest thine hand unto; and he shall bless thee in the land which the Lord thy God giveth thee. **9** The Lord shall establish thee an holy people unto himself, as he hath sworn unto thee, if thou shalt keep the commandments of the Lord thy God and walk in his ways. **10** And all people of the earth shall see that thou art called by the name of the Lord;

and they shall be afraid of thee. <sup>11</sup> And the LORD shall make thee plenteous in goods, in the fruit of thy body, and in the fruit of thy cattle, and in the fruit of thy ground, in the land which the LORD sware unto thy fathers to give thee. <sup>12</sup> The LORD shall open unto thee his good treasure, the heaven to give the rain unto thy land in his season, and to bless all the work of thine hand: and thou shalt lend unto many nations, and thou shalt not borrow. <sup>13</sup> And the LORD shall make thee the head, and not the tail; and thou shalt be above only, and thou shalt not be beneath; **if that thou hearken unto the commandments of the LORD thy God**, which I command thee this day, to observe and to do them: <sup>14</sup> And thou shalt not go aside from any of the words which I command thee this day, to the right hand, or to the left, to go after other gods to serve them.

Hearing God may not seem supernatural to some people, but it is! Please listen to my plea! *Hear and obey the voice of God,* and God will keep the river of blessings open into your life!

# 19

# March/April 1990:
# Gulf War Is Imminent

In a dream, I was taken above earth and heaven and shown in a vision the coming Gulf War and the region it would affect. I became a watchman. I warned! No one listened! It came to pass! My family has been blessed.

Ezekiel 33:1-7 (KJV)
Again the word of the LORD came unto me, saying, **2** Son of man, speak to the children of thy people, and say unto them, When I bring the sword upon a land, if the people of the land take a man of their coasts, and **set him for their watchman**: **3** If when he seeth the sword come upon the land, he blow the trumpet, and warn the people; **4** Then whosoever heareth the sound of the trumpet, and taketh not warning; if the sword come, and take him away, his blood shall be upon his own head. **5** He heard the sound of the trumpet and took not warning; his blood shall be upon him. But he that taketh warning shall deliver his soul. **6** But if the watchman see the sword come, and blow not the trumpet, and the people be not warned; if the sword come, and take any person from among them, he is taken away in his iniquity; but his blood will I require at the watchman's hand. **7** So thou,

O <u>son of man</u>, **I have set thee <u>a watchman</u>** unto the house of Israel; therefore thou shalt hear the word at my mouth, and warn them from me.

Hebrews 11:7 (KJV)

**7** By faith Noah, being **warned** of God of things not seen as yet, <u>moved with fear</u>, <u>prepared an ark</u> **to the saving of his house**; by the which he condemned the world, and became heir of the righteousness which is by faith.

In the dream, I was watching an airplane do aerial writing. I do not remember the words. While observing the airplane, I was taken high above the earth over the Persian Gulf. My attention was first drawn to the northernmost part of the Persian Gulf, to Kuwait, which became the doorway of coming wars. As I was looking down to Kuwait, it seemed as if a person was standing to my right side and extended a finger toward Kuwait and said, "War will break-out here." Then the same finger that pointed toward Kuwait drew a circle around the region from where Kuwait touches the Persian Gulf. The radius of the circle extended to the vicinity of Cairo Egypt, Cyprus, Eastern Turkey, very western edges of Afghanistan and Pakistan, and I believe all of Saudi Arabia.

I do not remember seeing Europe or India within the circle. I am not an expert in geography but quickly after having such visions, while the vision is clear, I review maps of the region to try to locate the nations and their borders. I did not hear the name of or the time of the war but only the warning of a coming war.

Then my focus shifted and narrowed to the north and west. All of Great Britain, the British Isles, was removed from the earth. The northern parts of France, Belgium, and the Netherlands no longer existed, and a fire was burning slowly down through the remaining portions of the three countries. I was concerned a blast had occurred in Great Britain and radiated beyond the English Channel. After seeing the vision, I ascended higher into the heavens until the earth disappeared from my sight.

I shared the vision, and many thought it was a revival among the Muslim nations, but I declared it as I saw it. Hopefully, the gospel of Jesus Christ will break-out among the majority of the Muslims, but the war did come under the name of "The Gulf War," and thus far, most of the destruction has been inside the circle. In August 1990, the United States began sending war preparations and the Gulf War ended by the end of February 1991.

Since the vision, the United States has suffered several Muslim driven attacks. Bombings, mass murders, are the most common thus far. The 911 attack in 2001 was the most destructive, but that may not be the worst if we fail to hear and obey God. God has sent many warnings through many people. If we heed the warning and take the appropriate action, we can be spared more tragedies.

Hopefully, my latest revelation of the part concerning Great Britain is that Ireland will explode with the glory of God and spread the gospel across Europe, even back to Paul's entry point at Macedonia.

# 20

# December 17, 1990: A Cloud of Deadly Poisons

Several men that I recognized were farm laborers. We all dressed alike in blue jean work pants and blue chambray shirts. We worked together in a field once worked by machinery. No women were visible.

Our field boss warned us to take shelter in a nearby building. A cloud was approaching, and it was rumored to be full of deadly poison. A young person came forward with a computer print-out of the chemical analysis of the cloud. I did not recognize the names of the poisons, but some of their names ended with the letters (ene) and one with (fax). Multiple thousands and possibly millions had been killed by the cloud's poisons.

The sky was full of airplanes of all types, shapes, and ages. One kind of plane was almost tear-drop in shape. Another unusual shape was that of a pot-belly minnow. I had seen both in earlier dreams. The planes flew at a low altitude and were easily recognized. A loud noise brought me out of the dream. I have not dwelt on this particular dream even though it may great significance. If the United States were to fall from a republic to a dictatorship, more manual labor would be the norm.

# 21

# 1993-1996:
# Tornadoes on the Prowl

The dreams began with one tornado per dream, but the number of tornadoes within the dream steadily increased. Shortly after the onset of the dreams, tornadoes were three abreast bearing down on me from every direction at the same time. It seemed the tornadoes were sent to kill me, but they were never able to harm me. The last and most significant dream of this series was in the spring of 1996. I do think it is odd that many of my dreams contain familiar geography.

I had left the farm, my dad's house, and was driving west on the gravel road, toward Dexter, Missouri. As I traveled, further along, more and more tornadoes were forming to the west. The number and intensity of the tornados were at their peak. The whole horizon was filled with tornadoes. I stopped the vehicle and got out for a better view. While looking southwest, everything became dark, and I realized I was in the path of a very large tornado. I fell, prostrate to the ground, my head facing the storm and my fingers clutching the earth. As the tornado passed over, I could feel it trying to lift me off the ground. It did not.

It passed without harming me. Then I stood up to study the horizon. What did I see? I saw innumerable tornadoes to the southwest, south, southeast, and east. The tornadoes were so numerous as if one was on every degree of a compass. It seemed like the whole world was under a tornado warning and no place to seek shelter. It was obvious to me that my life was being hunted by the powers of darkness. I was puzzled but not scared. Throughout the vision, I did not look to the North or east, the area of my assignment since 1982. It was not until I turned to the east that I perceived the glory of God coming to rescue me.

As I was facing east, I stopped as I saw a different looking cloud in the midst of the storms. It was shaped somewhat like an incandescent light bulb. It was not dark like the tornadoes. It was translucent and full of electricity and lightning. Unlike a lightning storm, none of the energy went beyond the border of the cloud. I continued to stare at the cloud until I realized it was moving toward me.

> Ezekiel 1:4 (KJV)
> 4 And I looked, and, behold, a whirlwind came out of the north, a great cloud, and **a fire in-folding itself**, and a brightness was

about it, and out of the midst thereof as the colour of amber, out of the midst of the fire.

As the cloud of fire moved across the field towards me, I perceived that it was God coming in His glory. The fear of God overcame me, and I fell facedown to the ground in a fetal position. My body was drawn up tightly with my face against my knees and my arms and hands wrapped around my head. I was scared, and I made myself as small as possible in His presence. I heard the sound of the cloud, a hum, as it hovered over me. The cloud, full of a warm colored haze, similar to the cloud that I had entered after I had drowned in Milford Lake, July 11, 1971, no sound existed inside the cloud, not even voices.

My body began to ascend rapidly and continued to ascend while in the face down fetal position. As the ascension slowed, my body began to uncurl, and I was made to stand upright on my feet, facing the east. I did not stand up on my own power. As soon as I was fully standing, a voice spoke from above and simultaneously a large window or movie screen opened in the east. I saw an army of soldiers moving from my right to my left. They were armed for war and were moving north and east. The soldiers were wearing tricorne hats, similar to the ones worn during the Revolutionary War of the United States of America. As the sound of the words faded, the vision ended. I was so terrified during this vision I do not know what was said to me.

Though I did not get the message that day, I believe it has been revealed day by day as I continue in ministry. I have not been sent to a strange people. Most of my assignment is to the household of God. When I go into areas unfamiliar with the gospel message, I am received, and the people respond to the goodness of God. The broken of this world are looking for a way out of their mess. The church is looking for a way to hold on to its mess, the traditions of men. I will continue my assignment among both groups and bear fruit as I can.

Ezekiel 1:28 (KJV)

28 As the appearance of the bow that is in the cloud in the day of rain, so was the appearance of the brightness round about. This was the appearance of the likeness of **the glory of the Lord**. And <u>when I saw it</u>, <u>I fell upon my face</u>, and <u>I heard a voice of one that spake</u>.

Ezekiel 2:1-10

And he said unto me, <u>Son of man, stand upon thy feet, and I will speak unto thee</u>. 2 And <u>the spirit entered into me</u> when he spake unto me, <u>and set me upon my feet</u>, that I heard him that spake unto me. 3 And he said unto me, Son of man, I send thee to the children of Israel, to a rebellious nation that hath rebelled against me: they and their fathers have transgressed against me, even unto this very day. 4 For they are impudent children and stiffhearted. I do send thee unto them; and thou shalt say unto them, Thus saith the Lord God. 5 And they, whether they will hear, or whether they will forbear, (for they are a rebellious house,) yet shall know that there hath been a prophet among them. 6 And thou, son of man, **be not afraid of them**, **neither be afraid of their words**, though briers and thorns be with thee, and thou dost dwell among scorpions: be not afraid of their words, **nor be dismayed at their looks**, though they be a rebellious house. 7 And thou shalt speak my words unto them, whether they will hear, or whether they will forbear: for they are most rebellious. **8** But thou, son of man, hear what I say unto thee; Be not thou rebellious like that rebellious house: open thy mouth, and eat that I give thee. **9** And when I looked, behold, an hand was sent unto me; and, lo, a roll of a book was therein; **10** And he spread it before me; and it was written within and without: and there was written therein lamentations, and mourning, and woe.

Through the telling of these dreams and visions, it has become evident that God has opened the north and east to me. I am a part of an army of God to do ministry within the portion of the earth revealed to me in 1982, the north and the east in the United States and north and west Europe. Any other direction is filled with storms of life that intend my harm. I can miss these storms if I hear and obey God. Thank God, God has delivered me from my ignorance to continue in my calling and assignment!

Ezekiel 3:1-8

Moreover, he said unto me, Son of man, eat that thou findest; eat this roll, and go speak unto the house of Israel. **2** So I opened my mouth, and he caused me to eat that roll. **3** And he said unto me, Son of man, cause thy belly to eat, and fill thy bowels with this roll that I give thee. Then did I eat it; and it was in my mouth as honey for sweetness. **4** And he said unto me, Son of man, go, get thee unto the house of Israel, and speak with my words unto them. **5** For thou art not sent to a people of a strange speech and of an hard language, but to the house of Israel; **6** Not to many people of a strange speech and of an hard language, whose words thou canst not understand. Surely, <u>had I sent thee to them, they would have hearkened unto thee</u>. **7** <u>But the house of Israel will not hearken unto thee; for they will not hearken unto me: for all the house of Israel are impudent and hardhearted</u>. **8** Behold, I have made thy face strong against their faces, and thy forehead strong against their foreheads.

Possibly this dream is more confirmation of the glory of God working through my life. Paul reveals to the Corinthians that we **are changed into the same image of God from glory to glory, even as by the Spirit of the Lord.** Paul declares to Timothy that we are to endure hardness as a good soldier.

As did Old Testament prophets, I wrestle with the desire to receive man's approval, but I am committed to obey in my assignment, even if I am never received. In the open vision of 1982, I saw my assignment to the North and East in the United States of America and over into Europe as far East as the Eastern border of Finland.

This supernatural ministry is bizarre and most often rejected by the modern-day Church. I am very thankful for my supernatural life! Since it has been with me for at least 65 years, I cannot imagine living without it. In my life, it is a daily choice to hear and obey God or yield to the traditions of men. In my ignorance, I have been somewhat like Jonah and run from my assignment. I am glad to be back on track. As for me and my house, we will obey the Lord and be blessed!

# 22

# Spring of 1996:
# The Most Terrifying Fire

In the dreams of tornadoes, I would often see to the west. In the last dream of the previous dreams, the whole western hemisphere was full of tornadoes. In this dream, the most terrifying dream of this series, the west was void of any physical definition. It appeared to be flat and black, maybe like a jeweler's cloth. From this very black background, God displayed his most terrifying warning to the United States.

As I stared at the unusual sight of a blackened hemisphere, a vision began to form. I noticed that the curtain of black began to move as if it was catching a wind. Have you seen the wind fill the sail of a ship and move the ship across the water? Have you seen the wind move clothes on a clothesline until they are dry? Something was beginning to move the dark curtain. I was very curious as to what would be causing the movement. I stared very intently, looking for the power causing the movement.

As the movement increased, I noticed an amber color developing within the blackness. As the amber color intensified, it had the appearance of a large petroleum fire. A large petroleum fire produces a blackness of smoke boiling together with the flame of fire burning the petroleum. Suddenly, all the blackness disappeared, and the whole western hemisphere was a total fame of fire.

The fire began to close over the whole canopy of heaven. The fire moved like an eyelid closing over a person's eyeball or the cover of a round chafing dish covering the food. Ahead of the total canopy of fire were huge tongues of fire. These enormous tongues of fire were high in the heavens and many miles in advance of the body of fire. This fire was to the earth as the tongues of fire were to the 120 people in the upper room on the day of Pentecost.

> Acts 2:1-4 (KJV)
> And when the day of Pentecost was fully come, they were all with one accord in one place. **2** And suddenly there came a sound from heaven as of a rushing mighty wind, and it filled all the house where they were sitting. **3** And there appeared unto them **cloven tongues <u>like as of fire</u>**, and it sat upon each of them. **4** And they were all filled with the Holy Ghost and began to speak with other tongues, as the Spirit gave them utterance.

As the tongues of fire passed over the earth, many things on earth instantly turned to ash. All things that were destroyed turned to ash without a flame being seen upon it. I do not remember any of the natural activities, sounds or smell of a fire. It was instant incineration of whatever was touched by the fire! Some of the ash heaps had no smoke, but some did leave trails of smoke. Even things hidden under the soil [stubble that had been plowed under] would turn to ash. When these hidden things burned, their location was revealed by the rivulets of smoke coming up out of the earth.

Many things remained intact as the tongues of fire passed over the earth. Nothing survived the body of fire that followed the tongues of fire. It was an absolute inferno! It consumed everything in its path. At least that was my perception because the body of fire was so intense, I could not see into it. My daughter Sarah was with me in the vision, and I had grabbed her and jumped upon the flatbed of a service truck. We survived the tongues of fire without harm, and we were terrified by the oncoming body of fire.

The only flame of fire that I saw on the ground was a small flame of fire burning on the vehicle's transmission. The transmission had an oil leak, and a small flame was burning upon that oil. The body of fire was moving at a tremendous speed. Life as we had known it was ending in the twinkling of an eye. The vision ended as the body of fire was not many miles to our west.

> Jeremiah 21:11-14 (KJV)
> **11** And touching the house of the king of Judah, say, Hear ye the word of the LORD; **12** O house of David, thus saith the LORD; Execute judgment in the morning, and deliver him that is spoiled out of the hand of the oppressor, **lest <u>my fury</u> go out *like fire*, and <u>burn</u> that <u>none can quench it</u>**, because of the evil of your doings. **13** Behold, I am against thee, O inhabitant of the valley, and rock of the plain, saith the LORD; which say, Who shall come down against us? or who shall enter into our habitations? **14** But I will punish you according to the fruit of your doings, saith the LORD: and **<u>I will kindle a fire</u>** in the forest thereof, and it shall devour all things round about it.

In recent decades, a shroud of darkness has been gradually pulled over the church. This shroud needs to be removed from the church, and its light needs to be seen. First, the lamp bowl, the church and the spirits of men, must be filled with the oil of regeneration. Our souls are the wicks of the lamp and need to be dipped into and saturated with the oil. If we are not saturated with the oil, we will be lighted with much difficulty and not burn long.

The Lord will trim the wicks of the lamp to give the greatest amount of light to the world. Until the wick is properly trimmed, the lamp's flame will have a mixture of orange and black. After the wick is properly trimmed, the blackness will virtually disappear.

Hopefully, this vision is an indication of another awakening and empowering as on the day of Pentecost. Then we will break out among the unsaved to purify their hearts before God's judgment comes to earth. Even if this dream had nothing to do with a new awakening, every individual could see the need for new birth and cleansing of our lives before the great and awesome day of the Lord.

# 23

# Jan 1998:
# Lives Spared by Prayer

While preaching on a Sunday evening, a vision opened my heart to see the aftermath of a wreck. The occupants were out of the vehicle on the frozen ground crying out for help. I stopped the service immediately and shared with the congregation what I had just seen by vision. We joined together in prayer and intercession for a time. The prayer time was intense but short! We thanked God for the deliverance of the occupants involved in the wreck, and we continued the normal service.

Later in the night, in the early hours of Monday morning, my brother Joe and his two sons were involved in a vehicle accident. The accident occurred about one-quarter mile south of our church. It was a very cold winter night. I do not know the cause of the accident. The vehicle was destroyed, but the occupants were spared harm. They tried to contact me on their cell phone. I missed the call, but my brother Dan received the call and retrieved them to safety. God used a supernatural vision to reveal a disaster. He also used the supernatural power of prayer to create the safety net. This supernatural life should be the normal life of a Christian.

# 24

# March 2005:
# Hope of Revival in a Dry Land

I was raised up above the earth from Sikeston, Missouri. I saw all the area around Poplar Bluff, Missouri aglow as if it was on fire. I did not see intricate details inside the glow. I believed it was a coming revival. I shared the dream with a few people. At the time, very few who heard me believed it could be a revival. Over the last twelve years, more people are seeing by dreams and visions of the glory of God coming to southeast Missouri. Hopefully, this glory will bear the fruit of righteousness.

# 25

# July 18, 2005:
# Airline Passenger Spared

I was awakened early in the morning after seeing a jet airliner flying at a very dangerously low altitude. I did not see fire on the outside, but smoke appeared to be coming through the fuselage. It was flying in stormy conditions through broken clouds. I shared the dream at church, and the congregation spent time in prayer asking for the safety of the passengers and crew. Within a few days, a large jet airliner in Canada crashed on its second approach to land. It was flying in similar conditions seen in the dream. All the passengers were spared. Everyone escaped without major injury. It was reported as a miracle. God needs intercessors on the earth who will work with Him to spare lives from the enemy's strategies.

Many see the future but dismiss it as their imagination. All of us should take our position of responsibility and cooperate with the Holy Spirit. God has good planned for people even if they are not Christians. God spared my life many times before I became a Christian and you as well. Let us help God deliver people from death.

# 26

# 2017 September 2: Atomic Explosion Revealed

I was doing my one-hour Holy Ghost Prayer Meeting and about 4:40 PM I saw a mushroom cloud come up out of the ground. I held what I saw for a few minutes before mentioning it to the prayer audience. I said, "A nuclear bomb has been detonated or will be in the near future, and our prayers are for their protection."

What I mentioned on Facebook Live Holy Ghost Prayer Meeting came to pass. Within six hours, North Korea exploded a hydrogen bomb underground. I am convinced that God wants to show us even more than we have ever seen. He desires people to take it to prayer and intercession. We should pray until we are convinced we have received the answer. We will recognize that God has released from further need to pray for that situation.

# 27

# Revealed but Not Delivered

Even though we see many things by vision and cooperate with God in prayer and intercession, we do not control the outcome. At various times I have been shown people in adultery. I prayed they would come to their senses and turn away from the sin. I did obey God. I did pray. They did not change. Did I miss God? Was my prayer ineffective? No! I do not know why they continued with the sin, but I do know I have no control over another person's will. Some of the marriages ended in divorce, and others remained intact with much pain and sorrow.

# 28

# Accident Avoided by Unseen Force

My wife and I have had a near car accident where she should have been hit in the front door, but the oncoming vehicle was moved immediately to the other side of us. Did the vehicle supernaturally pass through us, go over us, or go around us? We are not fully persuaded of how we were supernaturally delivered. We do know that Harriet was calling on the name of the Lord, screaming, "Jesus! Jesus! Jesus!" We have been delivered from other near accidents and death in actual accidents as she called upon the Name of The Lord.

Other than that, I offer no speculative conclusion. Maybe angels supernaturally moved the vehicles. It is no stranger than angels removing me out from under the falling building and the falling truck. We do not have a definitive explanation for the blessing; only that we are very thankful that we are alive and unharmed to share it.

# Summary

I have recorded some of the dreams and visions that have been significant in my life. Many things have not been recorded here, but I pray that it has been enough to stimulate you to reconsider your own dreams and visions. You can see from what I have shared that I do not have a full understanding of all that I have seen, but I hold it dear as it may be revealed in the future.

God desires to lead us into all truth and show us things to come. Please review Scriptures about dreams and visions. Pay attention to both purpose and benefit from understanding and obeying a dream. Some dreams and visions will not be clearly understood when you receive them. Do not discard the dream or vision as it may have significance later in life. Déjà vu means something already seen. When you enter a life situation, God may bring back to your remembrance something He has shown you earlier to prepare you for the moment at hand.

# Scriptural Evidence for Predictive Prophecy Today

     I hold that prophets today are also *seers* as in the Old Testament. Today, we surely have prophets of forth-telling but have never lost the need of the prophets of foretelling. Forth-telling, fore-telling and the accuracy of both are revealed in 2 Chronicles 20:14-29.

> 2 Chronicles 20:14-29 (KJV)
> <sup>14</sup>Then upon Jahaziel the son of Zechariah, the son of Benaiah, the son of Jeiel, the son of Mattaniah, a Levite of the sons of Asaph, came the Spirit of the LORD in the midst of the congregation;

Verse15-16 is the <u>Fore-Telling</u> which is answered in vs. 22-24.

> <sup>15</sup>And he said, Hearken ye, all Judah, and ye inhabitants of Jerusalem, and thou king Jehoshaphat, Thus saith the LORD unto you, Be not afraid nor dismayed by reason of this great multitude; for the battle is not yours, but God's.
> <sup>16</sup>Tomorrow go ye down against them: behold, they come up by the cliff of Ziz; and ye shall find them at the end of the brook, before the wilderness of Jeruel.
> <sup>17</sup>Ye shall not need to fight in this battle: set yourselves, stand ye still, and see the salvation of the LORD with you, O Judah and Jerusalem: fear not, nor be dismayed;

tomorrow go out against them: for the LORD will be with you.

¹⁸ And Jehoshaphat bowed his head with his face to the ground: and all Judah and the inhabitants of Jerusalem fell before the LORD, worshipping the LORD.

¹⁹ And the Levites, of the children of the Kohathites, and of the children of the Korhites, stood up to praise the LORD God of Israel with a loud voice on high.

Verse 20 is Forth-Telling answered in vs. 27-29.

²⁰ And they rose early in the morning and went forth into the wilderness of Tekoa: and as they went forth, Jehoshaphat stood and said, <u>Hear me, O Judah, and ye inhabitants of Jerusalem; Believe in the LORD your God, so shall ye be established; believe his prophets, so shall ye prosper.</u>

²¹ And when he had consulted with the people, he appointed singers unto the LORD, and that should praise the beauty of holiness, as they went out before the army, and to say, Praise the LORD; for his mercy endureth forever.

Verses 22-24 is the Answer to the Fore-Telling in vs16.

²² And when they began to sing and to praise, the LORD set ambushments against the children of Ammon, Moab, and mount Seir, which were come against Judah; and they were smitten.

<sup>23</sup> For the children of Ammon and Moab stood up against the inhabitants of mount Seir, utterly to slay and destroy them: and when they had made an end of the inhabitants of Seir, every one helped to destroy another.

<sup>24</sup> And when Judah came toward the watch tower in the wilderness, they looked unto the multitude, and, behold, they were dead bodies fallen to the earth, and none escaped.

<sup>25</sup> And when Jehoshaphat and his people came to take away the spoil of them, they found among them in abundance both riches with the dead bodies, and precious jewels, which they stripped off for themselves, more than they could carry away: and they were three days in gathering of the spoil, it was so much.

<sup>26</sup> And on the fourth day they assembled themselves in the valley of Berachah; for there they blessed the LORD: therefore the name of the same place was called, The valley of Berachah, unto this day.

Verse 27-29 is the answer to forth-telling in vs. 20.

<sup>27</sup> Then they returned, every man of Judah and Jerusalem, and Jehoshaphat in the forefront of them, to go again to Jerusalem with joy; for the LORD had made them to rejoice over their enemies.

<sup>28</sup> And they came to Jerusalem with psalteries and harps and trumpets unto the house of the LORD.

²⁹ And the fear of God was on all the kingdoms of those countries when they had heard that the LORD fought against the enemies of Israel.

Daniel of the Old Testament and John of the New Testament saw many future events and recorded what they saw. Neither prophet elaborated beyond what they understood. Many scholars today argue over the meanings of those prophecies. Current interpretations do not validate nor invalidate the recordings of either prophet. Please consider interpretations are speculative. It is okay to dig for revelation but do not forsake living by the revealed that has been proven. Using intellect to unveil hidden meaning is good. However, receiving revelation by the Holy Ghost is better.

In the New Testament, Jesus promised that the Holy Spirit would show us things to come.

John 16:13 (KJV)
¹³ Howbeit when he, the Spirit of truth, is come, he will guide you into all truth: for he shall not speak of himself; but whatsoever he shall hear, that shall he speak: and he will shew you things to come.

The prophet Agabus, being among other prophets at Antioch, spoke of a future famine. The church believed the prophet and things prophesied were established. The predictive prophecy had stirred believers to set aside some money every week to meet the needs in a future famine. The famine did come to pass, and the need was met for those affected by the famine.

Acts 11:27-30 (KJV)
²⁷ And in these days came prophets from Jerusalem unto Antioch. ²⁸ And there

stood up one of them named Agabus and signified by the Spirit that there should be great dearth throughout all the world: which came to pass in the days of Claudius Caesar. **29** Then the disciples, every man according to his ability, determined to send relief unto the brethren which dwelt in Judaea: **30** Which also they did, and sent it to the elders by the hands of Barnabas and Saul.

Jehoshaphat's encouragement holds true today, *"Believe the prophets and be established."*

2 Chronicles 20:20b
<u>Hear me, O Judah, and ye inhabitants of Jerusalem; Believe in the LORD your God, so shall ye be established; believe his prophets, so shall ye prosper</u>.

Dreams and visions are some of God's methods of communicating to man. We must not follow psychics, palm readers or those who commune with the dead, but we must follow the Scriptures and the Holy Spirit. There is safety in Him.

I am currently seeking further revelation of my aforementioned dreams and visions as I believe it is possible they affect a greater audience beyond my personal space.

I hold that all the Ephesian 4:11 gifts are to reveal Jesus Christ to this world. I have no gift to rule over anyone. As a minister of the gospel message of Jesus Christ, I am responsible (1) to preach my highest revelation of Jesus, (2) to lead others to seek Him for their own greater revelation of the person Jesus Christ.

Ephesians 1:15-23 (KJV)

15 Wherefore I also, after I heard of your faith in the Lord Jesus, and love unto all the saints, 16 Cease not to give thanks for you, making mention of you in my prayers; 17 That the God of our Lord Jesus Christ, the Father of glory, may give unto you the spirit of wisdom and revelation in the knowledge of him: 18 The eyes of your understanding being enlightened; that ye may know what is the hope of his calling, and what the riches of the glory of his inheritance in the saints, 19 And what is the exceeding greatness of his power to us-ward who believe, according to the working of his mighty power, 20 Which he wrought in Christ, when he raised him from the dead, and set him at his own right hand in the heavenly places, 21 Far above all principality, and power, and might, and dominion, and every name that is named, not only in this world, but also in that which is to come: 22 And hath put all things under his feet, and gave him to be the head over all things to the church, 23 Which is his body, the fulness of him that filleth all in all.

Philippians 3:10 (KJV)

10 **That I may know him**, and the power of his resurrection, and the fellowship of his sufferings, being made conformable unto his death;

2 Timothy 1:12 (KJV)

12 For the which cause I also suffer these things: nevertheless, I am not ashamed: for **I know whom I have believed** and am

persuaded that he is able to keep that which I have committed unto him against that day.

# Dr. David Craig
# Gift/Calling Mix for Ministry

Prophecy/Teaching/Exhortation

Romans 12:3-8 (KJV)
3 For I say, through the grace given unto me, to every man that is among you, not to think of himself more highly than he ought to think; but to think soberly, according as God hath dealt to every man the measure of faith. 4 For as we have many members in one body, and all members have not the same office: 5 So we, being many, are one body in Christ, and every one members one of another. 6 Having then <u>gifts differing according to the grace that is given to us</u>, whether **prophecy**, let us prophesy according to the proportion of faith; 7 Or **ministry**, let us wait on our ministering: or he that teacheth, on teaching; 8 Or he that **exhorteth**, on exhortation: he that **giveth**, let him do it with simplicity; he that **ruleth**, with diligence; he that sheweth **mercy**, with cheerfulness.

Prophecy/Word of Wisdom/Word of Knowledge

1 Corinthians 12:4-11(KJV)
4 Now there are diversities of **gifts**, but the same Spirit. 5 And there are differences of **administrations**, but the same Lord. 6 And there are diversities of **operations**, but it is

135

the same God which worketh all in all. **7** But the manifestation of the Spirit is given to every man to profit withal. 8 For to one is given by the Spirit <u>**the word of wisdom**</u>; to another <u>**the word of knowledge**</u> by the same Spirit; 9 To another **faith** by the same Spirit; to another the **gifts of healing** by the same Spirit; 10 To another the **working of miracles**; to another **prophecy**; to another **discerning of spirits**; to another **divers kinds of tongues**; to another **the interpretation of tongues**: 11 But all these worketh that one and the selfsame Spirit, dividing to every man severally as he will.

Apostle/Prophet/Teacher

1 Corinthians 12:28 (KJV)
28 And God hath set some in the church, first **apostles**, secondarily **prophets**, thirdly **teachers**, after that miracles, then gifts of healings, helps, governments, diversities of tongues.

Ephesians 4:11 (KJV)
11 And he gave some, **apostles**; and some, **prophets**; and some, **evangelists**; and some, **pastors** and **teachers**;

# Dr. David Craig Commission for Ministry/Service

This was given to me in May 1979. My brother Danny, who was the pastor of Victory Temple, One Mile Road, Dexter, Missouri, asked if I had anything to say to the congregation. I answered no. However, the Holy Ghost was encouraging me to say something. He told me to go to pulpit read these two verses, say it applied to me and sit down. I did obey, and they remain the foundation of my service.

> Luke 4:18-19 (KJV)
> **18** The Spirit of the Lord is upon me, because he hath anointed me to preach the gospel to the poor; he hath sent me to heal the brokenhearted, to preach deliverance to the captives, and recovering of sight to the blind, to set at liberty them that are bruised, **19** To preach the acceptable year of the Lord.

Luke 4:18-19

1. to preach the gospel to the poor;
2. he hath sent me to heal the brokenhearted,
3. to preach deliverance to the captives,
4. and recovering of sight to the blind,
5. to set at liberty them that are bruised,
6. to preach the acceptable year of the Lord.

# Dr. David Craig
# Vision for Ministry

I am to teach and train the body of Christ to **become a success in this life in Christ Jesus**. Jesus is the foundation of all life. He upholds all things by the word of his power. He has given us access to everything he inherited. He has promised to us any portion of his inheritance that we are willing to homestead.

> Joshua 1:8 (KJV)
> **8** This book of the law shall not depart out of thy mouth; but thou shalt meditate therein day and night, that thou mayest observe to do according to all that is written therein: for then thou shalt make thy way prosperous, and then thou shalt have good success.

Move the body of Christ toward maturity in the image of Jesus Christ. Humans were created in His image and His likeness to manage earth just like He would manage it if He was managing it Himself.

> Romans 8:29 (KJV**)**
> 29 For whom he did foreknow, he also did predestinate to be conformed to the image of his Son, that he might be the firstborn among many brethren.

Emphasize the necessity to bring our flesh into submission to Christ Jesus and to transform our lives to think and act like Jesus Christ through continual mind renewal. We are both outward and inward in our human construction. We are a triune being, spirit, soul, and body. Our spirit and soul make up our inward man and cannot be separated but only distinguished, and that only by the Word of God.

Romans 12:1-2 (KJV)
I beseech you therefore, brethren, by the mercies of God, that ye present your bodies a living sacrifice, holy, acceptable unto God, which is your reasonable service. 2 And be not conformed to this world: but be ye transformed by the renewing of your mind, that ye may prove what is that good, and acceptable, and perfect, will of God.

# About the Author

Dr. David Craig, Pastor of Life Church, is a graduate of the University of Mississippi with degrees in Biology, Psychology, and Chemistry. David completed a tour of duty in the U.S. Army and farmed before founding David Craig Ministries and Life Church. He received his Associate of Practical Theology and Bachelor of Pastoral Theology from Golden Grain Bible Seminary in 1992. He was awarded an Honorary Doctorate of Divinity from Midwest Theological Seminary in 2003 in recognition for the extensive work and support given in establishing international sites for training pastors. He serves on the Board of Directors for the American Mission Teams and of International Institute of Bible Theology of Central and South America. Life Church was the founding church of the ICBT program in the United States in 1990. He has a love for the mission field. He is received as a father to many and is ever ready to strengthen the pastor and church on the front line of the battlefield against the enemy.

David Craig began broadcasting over the radio in 1979 and television in 1983. God's Class on television and radio helps to equip the saints for effective and fruitful service in the kingdom. He is a passionate defender of the faith and believes that the gospel will change the life of any man, woman, or child who will receive and act upon it. Noted for his prophetic insight, the gifts of the Holy Ghost are given free reign and expression through this yielded vessel. Many people have been blessed, encouraged and built up in the faith by applying the practical principles of Christian living emphasized through the teaching ministry of Dr. David Craig.

Dr. David Craig is also the author of **"Why Should I Speak in Tongues?"** Published December 2017.

To order additional copies of this book or for further information, please contact:

Life Church
PO Box 1652
Sikeston, Mo 63801

573.471.6020 (office)
573.471.9182 (fax)
573.380.6993 (cell)

David@dcmlifechurch.org
www.dcraig.org
#dcm
#davidcraigministries
Davidcraigministries.yourstreamlive.com

98294022R00085

Made in the USA
Columbia, SC
22 June 2018